Bird's Nest Soup

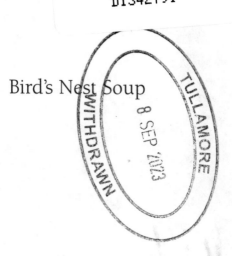

.e

íí mo
r nó r

ır iarra
thnuach

Gearrfaí
hoimeá

Bird's Nest Soup

HANNA GREALLY

Published in 2008 by Attic Press
Attic Press is an imprint of Cork University Press,
Youngline Industrial Estate, Pouladuff Road,
Togher, Cork, Ireland

First published in Ireland by Allen Figgis & Co 1971
Published in 1987 by Attic Press

British Library Cataloguing in Publication Data
A CIP catalogue record for this book is available from the British Library

ISBN 978-185594-210-3

Printed by Gutenberg Press, Malta

Contents

Foreword to 2008 edition	vii
Foreword to 1987 edition	xvii
Foreword to 1971 edition	xxi
Chapter 1	1
Chapter 2	6
Chapter 3	10
Chapter 4	15
Chapter 5	20
Chapter 6	25
Chapter 7	30
Chapter 8	35
Chapter 9	39
Chapter 10	44
Chapter 11	48
Chapter 12	53
Chapter 13	58
Chapter 14	63
Chapter 15	68
Chapter 16	73
Chapter 17	78
Chapter 18	83

Chapter 19	88
Chapter 20	92
Chapter 21	97
Chapter 22	102
Chapter 23	107
Chapter 24	111
Chapter 25	116
Chapter 26	120
Afterword to 1987 edition	125
Postscript	136
Afterword to 1971 edition	137

Foreword
to the 2008 edition

This re-publication of Hanna Greally's *Bird's Nest Soup* is a cause for celebration. Like many who read Hanna's story of eighteen years in St Loman's Psychiatric Hospital in its previous editions, I felt that it deserved a new life, a new form, and new audiences. To have lost this account of life inside the asylum would have been a small tragedy. For, while *Bird's Nest Soup* is one person's story, it also makes visible the many women and men who lived and sometimes died inside these institutions, often abandoned by family and society, often institutionalised to within inches of their lives. Just fifty years ago, in 1958, 21,000 Irish people were confined behind mental hospital walls – 0.7 per cent of the country's population. Most suffered what sociologist Erving Goffman called 'civil death':[1] the slow, stripping of personal identity, the ritualised mortification of the self to satisfy institutional needs. If Goffman had sought an exemplary story, he could have looked no further than *Bird's Nest Soup*. For this reason alone, *Bird's Nest Soup* deserves to be brought to a new generation.

There are other reasons too for welcoming its re-publication. It fills a gap in our social history about the worlds that existed inside these walls. If it is also a story of the abandonment of one woman into the psychiatric services at a time when single women without income or property were considered burdensome, it contributes to Irish women's history too.

That she was writing out of her own life does not preclude Hanna Greally writing in the lives of many others from occluded realms of the Irish historical experience. It could be said that Hanna's life's work was to reveal the hidden as will be seen in her two other manuscripts, to be published also by Cork Univeristy Press. In *Coolamber Manor* we get an insider's view of the Rehabilitation Centre in County Longford, where Hanna went after St Loman's and from where she hoped to gain freedom 'prodigously and for ever'. In 'Housekeeper at Large' she takes us into the life of an Irish woman as cook and housekeeper in homes and institutions in England throughout the 1960s.

A question remains, however, as to how we can make sense of what is a very idiosyncratic, highly personalised narrative written in a style which is out of favour today. When asked to write this Foreword I wondered what today's readers might make of *Bird's Nest Soup*. What meanings can it bring? Is it just a good story? Is it social commentary, literature?

It seems to me, first of all, that some biographical detail from Hanna's life would helpfully illuminate her work's meaning. Because, while *Bird's Nest Soup* is a very thinly disguised autobiography she set out to write novels and there is much she does not reveal about herself and her circumstances. But it is virtually impossible today to read this book without desiring more insight into the life of the narrator.

Hanna Greally was born in Athlone in 1925, on the western side of the Shannon, into a solidly middle-class business family. She was christened Johanna, called Joan throughout her life and chose Hanna as her writerly-name. The family business (a bar and grocery trade and other property) came through Hanna's mother Baby Murray (pronounced Mur-ray) who married James Greally, a salesman. Hanna and her brother enjoyed all the comforts of small-town middle-class Ireland – she played tennis, boated on the Shannon and went to the local fee-paying school, the Bower Convent. Her former neighbour, and later to become her adult friend, Eithne Quinn, recalls tea parties in the Greally house, complete with tea dresses for the ladies. Eithne still remembers Hanna and her mother as cutting fine figures around the town and Hanna's fame was sealed by the publication of her poetry in the town newspaper. The privileged early life proved vulnerable and

James' death, when Hanna was aged five began the incremental, slow undoing of the household and the business.

Hanna had hoped to become a teacher after her Leaving Certificate but family funds could not stretch to supporting her during training. Instead she took the boat to London to train as a nurse at Guy's Hospital. From this point, until Hanna appeared at the door of St Loman's some two years later, little in known about either Hanna's life or the family fortunes. We know that Hanna returned to Athlone in 1943 without completing her training. In Bird's Nest Soup she tells us that she wanted to be with her mother. There is an implication of loneliness and that Baby Murray herself needed nursing care. She describes finding much straightened family circumstances on her return. Those who got to know Hanna later in her life suggest also that the hospital where Hanna had been training was bombed during the Blitz and that she may have suffered somehow. Ultimately we can only speculate here. We might wonder, for instance, how Hanna's background and upbringing, the death of her father at a young age and her closeness to her mother, left her equipped to survive as a young Irish trainee nurse, in a wartime London hospital. Even in peacetime, trainee nursing was emotionally and physically tough, not for those with fanciful imaginations or strong wills. To return to find few of her childhood comforts still available to her must indeed have shaken her deeply.

From her writings and from some memories of those who knew Hanna – some of which are recorded in a recent radio documentary[2] – we know that some event after Hanna's return to Athlone resulted in Hanna entering St Loman's Psychiatric Hospital in nearby Mullingar for a 'rest'. Baby Murray signed her in. Bird's Nest Soup begins at this point, with Hanna at the door of the Admissions Ward. The tragic and disturbing story that followed constitutes the basis of the book. Eighteen years later Hanna finally emerged from St Loman's and, in turn, was one of the first participants in a new rehabilitation centre in Coolamber Manor, Longford.

Thanks to recent efforts, including the location of the manuscripts to be published, and renewed interest in Hanna's work we can now piece together more of her life from this point on. In *Coolamber Manor* Hanna details, with the same precision and careful representation evidenced in *Bird's Nest Soup*, the process that led to her full restoration to autonomy and citizenship. Here, Hanna trained alongside young women and emerged skilled and confident. The ten years or so that she spent after Coolamber in service in England constitutes the basis for the stories that unfold in 'Housekeeper at Large'.

But when and how did Hanna Greally, the writer, emerge from this life? We know that it was during her last years in England, when she found some semblance of a stable family life as a housekeeper for a retired doctor, 'Doctor Joseph', that Hanna began to write. We must assume that her writing received the support of the doctor and it is as if once Hanna began to draw from her own life, she could not stop. Here, Hanna wrote *Bird's Nest Soup*, and it is also likely that *Coolamber Manor* was completed, certainly begun, at this time.

Following the death of Dr Joseph in the late 1960s, Hanna returned to Ireland. With savings and money left to her she bought a small vested cottage a few miles outside Roscommon town, which she named 'Sunny Acre'. That she lived on her own is probably not surprising and we can imagine the pleasure she must have gained from being her own woman for the first time in her adult life. Her choice of location is a little surprising but, again, such a response occurs in a vacuum of knowledge. Did she, for instance, prefer rural isolation over town life? Why did she not return to Athlone? It may have been serendipity but, in fact, in choosing Roscommon she renewed a connection with her past and made new connections which were to prove vital for her later in life. Through the owner of a restaurant in Roscommon town she was reconnected with her old neighbour Eithne Quinn and, in turn, Eithne opened her circle of friends and her family to Hanna. It was these friends who celebrated with Hanna on the first publication of *Birds' Nest Soup*, by Allen and Figgis, in 1971, and supported her through the fame that followed – including an appearance on the 'Late Late Show'.

As viewers that night will have observed, Hanna was not shy. A perusal of the pages of the *Roscommon Champion* from this time reveals a woman who spoke out with relish, and frequently, on a range of topics. For instance, she took on a psychiatrist who challenged the veracity of *Bird's Nest Soup*. She engaged in a debate about the Irish flag. Her activities generated many news stories for the paper and over the years she contributed both letters and poetry; some were charming doggerel, and others lyrical and sensitive.

In 1972, the *Champion* serialised *Coolamber Manor* – advertising it in a strap headline as an instalment of 'a Johanna Greally book'.We are told that Hanna's third manuscript ('Housekeeper at Large') was awaiting publication. She appeared to be unstoppable.

Sadly, however, Hanna's writerly potential, evident from the work she produced at this time, was not to flourish. She earned little from the publication of *Bird's Nest Soup*. Neither of the other manuscripts were published in book form and 'Housekeeper at Large' never saw the light of day.

In fact, as recounted in the radio documentary, Hanna relied largely on friends to support her throughout the last decade of her life in 'Sunny Acre', and her final years were difficult. She was kind, lively and loyal to her friends. However, she was also a difficult person and it is not hard to imagine why. Her pride made her prickly about taking help and she asserted her independence even when it might not have been wise to do so. Her health was not good: she was a heavy smoker and bred dogs so her house and home life suffered accordingly. Neighbours brought her hot meals and she relied on lifts to get around.

In the early 1980s Hanna was hospitalised twice – for a heart operation and for surgery on her hand. In the end her general ill health took its toll and Hanna died in Roscommon County Hospital on 15 August 1987, aged just 62, weeks before the second publication of *Bird's Nest Soup* (by Attic Press). It is sad to think that Hanna could not enjoy her new audience and, in particular, an audience of women readers, who found echoes in it of their own lives.

That said, there are many enigmas at the heart of *Bird's Nest Soup* which do not diminish with time or with several readings.

When I first read the book in the 1980s, I was left with questions which took on their own power including the power to diminish the authenticity of the story. As readers slowly realise, the 'rest' for which Hanna entered St Loman's is euphemistic. As Hanna never explains why she was committed, we are left wondering. Perhaps its content rose from the imagination of a highly creative young woman who may indeed have been 'insane'? How can we, otherwise, make sense of the apparent cruelty of Baby Murray and the continuing heartlessness of Hanna's extended family who, she tells us, could have signed her out? Perhaps inside was the best place for Hanna, given the time: before the welfare state and patient rights? Some of Hanna's contemporaries, those who lived through the poverty and hardship of Ireland in the 1940s and 1950s, ventured to suggest to me that, for all its degradations, at least inside Hanna had three meals a day and a clean bed to sleep in each night. Harsh, yes, but is there something in not judging from the perspective of where we stand today? Or, if we wish to find someone to blame, to whom do we point our fingers? The family, wider society, the psychiatric profession, the institution?

Yet, one of the the cruellest moments in *Bird's Nest Soup* must surely be when, after some weeks inside, Hanna's mother tells her that her (Hanna's) room in the family home has been rented out. The bonds of family, however straightened, no longer extend to Hanna. Hanna's mother has become her jailer. How can we make sense of such a relationship, of such family breakdown? Again, we wonder whether Hanna's state of mental health was such that leaving her in the asylum was the only option. We can also wonder, however, if information about Hanna's mental health would in fact make any difference to the power of the story?

What did Hanna choose to tell us? Early in the book her mother advises her, following a consultation with the medics, that she had had a nervous breakdown. But, and here is the rub, Hanna comments that this must have happened 'by proxy'. There is a great deal of ambiguity here (perhaps deliberately) but I understand this comment to mean that the diagnosis, if not the breakdown itself, happened without Hanna's participation. It is as if Hanna is telling us that the psychiatrist and Baby Murray together agreed that she had a nervous breakdown and, moreover, Hanna is hinting – while all the time declaring love for her mother – that this somehow suited Baby Murray, who frets about her own health. It is as if Hanna came to realise that she was not wanted but could not name this directly. If this was true, Hanna was possibly in the 'right' place. Irish psychiatric institutions, like many elsewhere, were respositories for the mentally ill but also for the poor, the eccentric, the socially troublesome, the vulnerable and the unwanted.

Thus, while inevitably the power of the psychiatric institution dominates the book, it is the complex realtionship between Hanna and her mother which may also be a central story, albeit heavily veiled.

The lack of response from Hanna's extended family to her pleas for release is also deeply puzzling. An aunt, for instance, visits her in St Loman's and will not sign her out. Today, this seems inexplicable.

Here we might note the inexorable stigmatisation and fear of anyone with the taint of mental illness. That stigma was self-fulfilling. Once a person became a mental hospital inmate then the institution had the total power to label any behaviour (such as in Hanna's case, demands for her comfort) as evidence of instability. *Bird's Nest Soup* illustrates how this power was used to crush Hanna. Such institutions needed and, in turn perhaps, created the long-term insane. Moreover, psychiatric institutions in post-colonial Ireland were important places of income and employment. Perhaps it suited everyone to believe that those inside were rightly there. The experts, supported by the law, provided the rationale.

In truth, we will probably never fully grasp the complex web of interpersonal relationships and fears, and social and political forces that brought Hanna to the door of St Loman's and left her inside for almost twenty years. Part of the ineffable tragedy of the story, however, is that it took the arrival of a new superintendent in 1962, and new attitudes to mental health, to finally release her. Many others died inside before such change and it is clear from one very poignant passage in the book that Hanna was all too aware of those fates.

In the end, however, I suggest that *Bird's Nest Soup* is not at all about mental illness and that the question of Hanna's state of mind prior to entry is insignificant. It is a story about power and its abuse; a story of abandonment and brutal exclusion. It could, for instance, stand as a parable for bullying today.

To read this book is, I suggest, to primarily sink into the subjectivity of another, as she survives in a world that coexisted with, but was invisible to everyday Irish life in the recent past. It is to experience, at one remove, the ferocious institutionalised cruelty in the Irish mental hospital. It is a disturbing narrative of how a young woman becomes a person without autonomy or self-determination. We wilt at the grinding tedium over so many years and at the vast loss and grief. In Hanna's capaciousness for drama, intrigue and small pleasures, we get insight into how, despite such contexts, human beings always create social and ethical meaning for their lives. As she dignifies her fellow inmates with her intimate portrayals, we see that she is also redignifying herself.

Perhaps then we can accept *Bird's Nest Soup* not as great literature, but as literature that is important for its rich psychological and social insights which are, in turn, contemporary and universal. Readers can, I hope, also find this richness in their own responses. Most of all, this book invites us to think about power and its abuse, whether exercised by big institutions or by individuals, and about powerlessness and its impact on the human psyche.

While Hanna will not, clearly, witness this third edition of *Bird's Nest Soup*, nor the other books to follow, I have no doubt that her spirit is paying close attention. Cork University Press is to be congratulated for publishing these works and for re-introducing Hanna Greally, writer, to new audiences.

Dr Eilís Ward, School of Political Science and Sociology,
National University of Ireland, Galway

Notes and References

1 Goffman, Erving, 1961. *Asylums: Essays on the Social Situation of Mental Patients and other Inmates* (London: Penguin Books). See also Ward, Eilís, 2006. 'Security and Asylum: The Case of Hanna Greally' in *Studies*, Vol 95, No. 377: 65–76.
2 'Remembering Hanna Greally', Well Said Productions, first broadcast on Ros FM, 15 August 2007.

Foreword
to 1987 edition

What happens to a woman who is locked away for nearly twenty years? Can you visualise the pain, the loss of the most important time of your life? Imagine the anger and frustration of trying to cope with this when both your mind and body are sound? Is hate one of the emotions you feel when people say, 'it's for your own good'?

Hanna Greally was signed into the 'Big House' for a rest. Hers is a story of twenty years in a psychiatric hospital. Twenty years of being told what to do and when to do it. Twenty years of hard labour, unpaid hard labour. She writes about the days of the padded cell, insulin shock therapy and the 'big hole'. She recalls the early days of Electro Convulsive Therapy (ECT), when patients were given this treatment without an anaesthetic. She tells of being held down forcefully by three nurses as a doctor sent electric charges through her body. *Bird's Nest Soup* is Hanna's story and she tells it without emotion and with a simple clarity. It is what she does not tell us that haunts me.

How did a young articulate woman like her cope with the 'Big House'? She was there during the Second World War; was she afraid? Was she lonely? Did she regret the loss of possible relationships? How did she feel when her most fertile years began slipping away? Hanna missed the advent of television, the first man in space. Did anyone tell her who Yuri Gagarin was in 1957? What outside influences did she meet with? What was life like for her when she was freed in the early sixties? The strength that radiates from the pages of *Bird's Nest Soup* surely stood by Hanna Greally when she finally left the 'Big House'.

Meanwhile what about life in the 'Big House' eighties style? It's true to say some things have changed. We now have the Voluntary Patients Act; insulin therapy has gone the way of leeches and blood letting. No more hot and cold bath treatment; 'patients' are anaesthetised before receiving ECT; no more of the strait-jackets that Hanna talks about. We now have chemical strait-jackets and group therapy. Are these changes enough? While accepting that psychiatric hospitals are a necessary evil, I must question the numbers of people, especially women, who end up there. Is it really necessary? As one of those women who is a 'drop out' from the 'Big House' of the eighties I can only suspect the changes are *not* enough.

How did I, another young articulate woman, end up in a psychiatric hospital? Probably because I am a woman of my time, a victim of my gender. A woman who was despondently searching for herself in a patriarchal world. You'll find me everywhere. I'm listed in all the statistics. I'm a woman, working class, early school leaver, a separated mother and living on social welfare. I'm also one of the 'new poor' since I became a single mother. I'm also 'suspect' because of my 'illness' and the strain of having five children. But somewhere in all of this, I am me, trying to make sense of my life.

My own journey to the Big House was paved with unholy orders: barring orders, maintenance orders, family protection orders, not to mention attachment of earnings orders. I went on a pilgrimage of government buildings. I became the bearer of pink forms, blue forms and white and yellow forms. Nobody listened! They shot the messenger. I became an angry woman and society found me wanting. Women are supposed to be caring and passive, not angry.

Friends became worried; they suggested the doctor. I began another pilgrimage, of doctors, psychiatrists, therapists and counsellors. The memories become vivid again. They dole out pills by the fistful. I become less angry. I lose my appetite and my confidence. I 'pull myself together' as I do my daily round of housework, shopping, queuing at the clinic for supplementary welfare. I am accompanied on my travels by my five children.

These children don't like this new Mam. They don't like this calm robot-like woman.

Months pass and I'm still calm. I have found a way to exist. I stop talking and listening. I begin to live in my head. Someone calls the doctor. He sighs, tuts and asks, 'How did you get so low; what happened?' I scream and shout. Who needs him? I awake four days later in hospital. I'm brought to see a doctor. A psychiatrist. I sit there in my nightdress. He's wearing a three-piece suit. He's protected by this and by his huge desk. A woman sits in a corner; she writes down every thing I say. 'Who's she?' I ask. He doesn't answer. I walk out, back to bed and refuse their pills. A day passes; I try to come to terms with daily life in the female admission ward. There are lots of young mothers like me, all with similar stories. They are all suffering from depression, just like me. Is this hospital society's answer to people like us? None of the medical staff ever ask what can be done about the cause of our depression, they only ever talk about the depression itself and inevitably the answer always seems to be chemical incarceration. We are no longer, as was Hanna Greally, being held against our will for decades, but is the reality of drug oppression as bleak a future to face as twenty years in the 'Big House'?

Another day goes by. A social worker calls. This is the first time in my life ever to meet a social worker. He's male! He tells me about the family; the older kids are well. They're being looked after by neighbours. The twins have just gone into hospital. He says, 'It's nothing to worry about, just a chest infection.' This man then refuses to take me to see my babies. 'You need a rest.'

Shades of Hanna's story you think. Well unlike Hanna's story, my escape plans did succeed. Two days later I was home, and so were my twins. I found my anger again. This time I held on to it. I know I'm not a failure; it's society that's sick, not me. I'm no longer ashamed of living on the dole. I don't try to hide my poverty. I regret all those years of hiding behind my, 'I can cope' facade. Since I began to talk about being depressed, I find myself becoming part of a support network that's helping other women.

I have found some answers for myself. Many women find themselves depressed! It's a reactive depression caused by social difficulties. Narcosis is not the answer for women like us. Putting us into hospital won't solve anything. As Hanna says in her book, 'it's madness, but whose?'

Cathleen O'Neill, August 1987

Foreword
to 1971 edition

You forget only the things you want to forget, someone said. If I tried to visualise the whole of my twenty years' detention in an asylum, if I attempted to produce a 'ship's log' account of the day-to-day events, of the dreary hospital routine, it would be comparable to a hazy vision or a vast sea called memory, blurred by prevailing conditions, where people could pass for porpoises and porpoises for people, where Neptune's white head might rise in majesty, or bow sadly, as a white-haired prophet, without honour, where cabbages are kings and woman a spare rib. No, my thoughts revolve, and dwell for an instant or two, on more unforgettable aspects which I can remember at will.

I omit many incidents which, relatively, seem unimportant to me now. The years there seemed like eternity to me, and yet when I left they dropped from me like an old garment that I expect never to see again. The asylum is now called a mental hospital, so, to compromise between the sad, euphonious word, asylum, and the modern, physical-jerk words, mental hospital, I shall call this particular place – the Big House.

I went into the Big House an impulsive, uninhibited girl, and I left a cautious, subdued, almost servile woman. I am now a sadder but a wiser woman, and one who can say with certainty that knowledge and freedom are happiness.

Hanna Greally, 1971

Chapter 1

I was just over nineteen years of age when I was admitted as a patient to the Big House. I was one of three thousand patients then. The male admission wards and the female admission wards were one building, separated from each other by a narrow passage. One glass-topped door faced another glass-topped door, and the view down was cool, greenish, and restful to the eyes.

I sat on a chair beside the door. I stared down, remembering my mother's tears, her words of goodbye, and paid no attention to the man in the passage between the doors. The attendant with him opened the door of the male admission ward. They went in. I thought, another admission. I noticed he sat directly inside his door, like me, also staring out into the cool green passage, our last link with freedom. There were twelve panes of glass on each half-door, and I could now see his head and shoulders. He was about thirty, and his hair was red and long, like a girl's.

A male nurse came up the passage. He looked in, his eyes questing, and knocked. A nurse who had been writing in a report book looked up.

'There's an attendant at the door,' I said.

She let him in. They stood talking. He had come to borrow some surgical spirit for a tray, he said. It was only an excuse. He was her boyfriend. They arranged a meeting for later. I suddenly lost all interest and stared in front of me. It was all so terribly lonely here, I thought, so impersonal, cold.

The white coat's voice rose, laughing, yet insisting. 'You're all right, my new patient says he is Jesus Christ.' They both giggled.

'Honestly,' he said.

I was fascinated. I stared down at this strange man who claimed to be God. He stared back at me and I thought, perhaps he really is. He wore his clothes with a nomadic yet regal careless-ness. His answering stare spoke volumes – eternity in a glance, the angel stirring the waters, a whole vista of consolations I saw and felt in a flash. The admission or coming of this man, I thought, must not be without incident. I lost visual contact with him then, as the white coat left. When I looked down again he had gone. I wonder now if he is still there, if he protested when they cut his hair. Perhaps he too was forsaken like me, and when I think of him, I take courage. He also came into this strange world of the Big House the same day as I came, and then went out of my life. I might have met him hundreds of times after that, in the vastness of the Big House, shorn, shepherded, escorted by the white coats, but I cannot recall, because one only remembers what one wants to remember.

The superintendent of the Big House was tall, grey-haired and of the 'old school tie' variety; he had been an officer in the British army. He was distant, reserved, very evasive and non-committal. He dressed immaculately always, if rather fussily, and to all appear-ances of course he was, as most agreed, a distinguished and attractive man. By evasions and smiles he often raised spirits temporarily, and unnecessarily, for procrastination was both a friend and an enemy to him. Perhaps a month later, he would encounter the same irate mob demanding to know why their application for release had not only been discouraged, but rejected. He would just look hurt and remark: 'Tch! Tch!'

He also had many ready-made answers for the many nervous, floor-pacing patients who sought reassurance about going home.

'Ye-as, ye-as, certainly, at the next board meeting,' he would say.

In those days, all you needed, it seemed, was a letter from one responsible person, claiming you out. Those letters, for the majority, very rarely came.

I once asked him what he thought I was detained for, and he said I needed a rest after my 'nervous breakdown'. So that's it, I thought, now I wonder what Mother has said to him. I guessed she had used some well-worn cliché, but this was novel. Mother and I had agreed that I needed a rest, and that the Big House was the only place to go in the circumstances. Mother confessed that she had had some interviews with him on my behalf. Therefore I must assume I had a 'nervous breakdown' by proxy. Mother intimated also that I was complicated and difficult to diagnose. This was hardly her own opinion, which was that I was simple and easily led.

Once a year, on his rounds, the super was accompanied by a mental health inspector. The inspector would stop and talk to patients, and listen to 'complaints'. Many patients were so tired of complaining to the super that they often failed to recognise the true channel for complaint, and inexplicably they would ignore the inspector as not worth 'a go'.

One girl I knew complained, but trust the devil to take care of his own . . .

For one week she kept her uneaten portion of boiled meat in her locker awaiting the arrival of the inspector. When he arrived, she produced it to him, very excitedly, and asked him very sweetly, shoving it almost under his surprised nose, to tell her candidly, would he eat such horrible stuff; 'disgusting' was the word she used. She then claimed that this meat was an example of the nauseating stuff she was obliged to eat daily.

The matron and the inspector expressed disgust.

'Tch! Tch!' said the super, at which noise the matron signalled for Tessa to be removed from their path. Tessa was led away by the charge nurse to whom she offered her exhibit A, still excitedly discussing its obnoxious quality. The inspector immediately afterwards took out his little red book of complaints and made a note of it.

Tessa became very unpopular with the staff after that incident. She went on hunger strike for a day, but gave in when the nurses insisted on feeding her by hand from a dessert spoon. She had a delicate, flower-like, fragile face, and it was not a pretty sight, to see the fight between the spoon and Tessa's clenched, tiny, pearly teeth. The spoon won of course. Tessa never had a chance. She was like a kitten who instinctively used her claws, on the slightest pretext, just to see if they were developing. Before she succumbed to authority, and she did finally admit the impropriety of her act, under sedation, she spat tiny verbal insults at the food and the staff generally. One day, due to lack of sedation, she went too far. She slapped a nurse's face, and the nurse's sympathetic colleagues frogmarched her to bed. I hated to see Tessa so commonly used. She lay there in bed for six weeks thinking of her sin, of the slap, not sulkily, but exultantly. She was sweetly sarcastic to the nurses in general and, each time the super visited, she would stand up on the bed, excitedly trying to attract his attention, all the time demanding to know if her complaint had been lodged in the right quarters, and so on, until he finally hastened out to the dismissal she falsely prophesied for him.

The Big House was not just all grey walls, sheltering in its shadows the living breath. No! One can make a heaven of hell, if one is so inclined. I look outside, from my chair by the window, and I see the good green grass, inhale the wild perfume from the wallflower beds. If I open the window the full six inches, the scent, wafted gently in by the warm breeze, more than compensates for the boring vision of their tawny tatteredness. If I cross over the day-room to the opposite windows, more green fields, daffodil beds, and a view of a wood, outside the grounds, on the far horizon. A horse and rider, free, gallop through the wood in the mornings sometimes. If I could go now as far as the gatelodge I would pass the row of heavily laden lilac trees. In my mind I see the numerous little knolls where the crocus and the snowdrops grow. I see the unchanging symmetry of the super's rosebeds, his gardenias, his chrysanthemums and his purple- and yellow-flecked pansies.

There is a miniature wood where I once picked violets and snowdrops, an oasis, bordered by pine trees which continually scatter cones and pine needles underfoot. Further along is the chapel, a place of peace and prayer. A massive chestnut tree grows beside it, and regularly drops little and big spiked chestnuts long before the snows come. The great high red-brick furnace chimney further on, almost in the centre of the Big House acres, reaches up almost to the very clouds. An iron ladder goes right up to the top of it. A young man, barely thirty, jumped from it to his death once. Suicide, it was said.

If I keep going, I will see the abattoir, a chicken run, food stores, hardware stores, the upholstery shop, where mattresses are reteased. There is the shoe repair shop, and beside that, finally, the carpentry shop. The coffins are made there. I have often heard a patient say dispassionately: 'I'll only go out in "the box".'

Chapter 2

There was no voluntary status for inmates in the early 1940s. Lena arrived cyclically each year. Her dear advanced husband Jeff signed her in, not because he wanted to, she once remarked, but because he had to. She was an attractive woman, in a restless feline way. She had a thin tanned face, permed short brown hair. Her thin lips she carmined regularly and carefully. She always wore high-heeled shoes. They were part of her armoury. When she became really furious, and thought of Jeff's insensitive indifference to her physical and monetary demands, she would whip off a high-heeled shoe and attack one, or possibly two, of the twelve-inch window panes around us. Smash! Crack! Two more broken windows to add to the unaware rate-payers' burden.

On such occasions she always seemed unconcerned about the two or three nurses clinging to her like limpets, trying to restrain her. She would continue her tirade at the invisible Jeff, mocking him and his supposed defects, until finally she would cease the demonstration, and with a cunning twinkle in her eye, would seem to come to her senses. She would cling to the nurse, using an old infallible routine, making sobbing anguished sounds, as if she was just coming out of a nightmare, instead of being the creator of one. Then, submissively, she would be led away to her bed.

After nine months, usually, her attitude would change notice-ably, the novelty would wear off, and she would write a letter to Jeff, saying she felt well and would he mind claiming her out. The first sign was when she changed 'Jeff' to the elaborate 'Geoff'. She would speak of 'Jawf' then in the third person singular. She would say to us with a meaningful, victorious smile, 'Jawf is coming to take me home, girls.'

By 1960 her visits became more frequent. The reason for this, if reason it be, was that the Voluntary Patients Act came into force. Lena quickly availed of this innovation, and, tigress-like, she shot in and out approximately every six months. We could always tell when she arrived. If we were in bed at the time, we would recognise the shrill voice of Lena mocking, accusing, the absent, ever-patient Jeff. If she was not then put to bed before her tantrums developed, she would smash a window and hop into the ward holding her shoe, volubly explaining, perhaps to a new probationer, that she was a wronged woman, and explaining to a rather terrified nurse that men were beasts, leaving no doubt that she had an intimate knowledge of her beast above all beasts.

She was not so completely self-engrossed, though, as not to be baffled by my long, unbroken confinement. Once or twice concerning this, she attacked the staff, with her usual sarcastic derision, as to what I was doing there, that she would see to it, for she would expose the entire institution for unconstitutional practices.

I knew her, on and off, for almost twenty years in the Big House, and she was still the same Lena after twenty years – vital, temperamental, addicted to tantrums. Her eyes would flash, and would appear flecked, in one of her rages, then change to a dull butterscotch dark brown when her ego had been satisfied. She supplied an excitement for us; she made us aware of ourselves as women, and of our incalculable power over men.

In the middle ward of the admission, on a wild March night, a baby was born. It was on a Saturday, at 2am that we, in the adjacent darkened dormitory, heard the first cries. Through the glass partition which separated the dormitories, we saw the fuss, and watched the doctor arrive. Screens had been placed around the mother's bed, and we did not know who she might be.

'Shh!' said Miss Leather, 'something's up!'

We could not guess what it was all about until we heard the cries. Now, one bed was partially unscreened. The mother was

Sibyl; she was fifteen and unmarried. A nurse was attending her. The other nurse was standing by the bracketed night fire, cradling in her arms a tiny crying baby. It was wrapped in a soft creamy shawl. A huge open laundry basket with wicker handles was beside the fire. There was a new blanket in it. While we watched, the doctor went to the wash-basin, washed his hands and left.

One by one we made excuses to tiptoe in to have a look at the unexpected visitor. He had fair hair and blue eyes, as his mother Sibyl had. We had never suspected that Sibyl was pregnant. Like many women there, she wore no corset, and she also wore her coat in the daytime, when sometimes it could become very cold there. She never mentioned it once, and I doubt if she had known herself. She recovered quickly. In fact the next day she seemed glad, thankful and relieved when her baby was taken from her and sent to an orphanage run by nuns.

The staff maintained a discreet silence about the event afterwards, but not Sibyl. She laughed and joked about the event. She considered sex a game, a pleasant pastime, and she had not expected a baby. She worried just a little whether her parents would send her away to work and she would have to find other boyfriends.

'Poor child, only fifteen, she has no sense,' the older women said.

The young girls would gather around her and listen with gasping awe to intimate accounts by Sibyl of love scenes in love lanes and remote hay barns. After a week she was moved to Prospect House and I heard from there that her parents had taken her home.

One of my friends in the admission was Dorothy. We spent many hours together, laughing, talking, desperately trying to forget or hide our misery at being 'locked up'. I loved our chats. We used to pretend that we were somewhere else; for example, in a comfortable hotel lounge. Little did I know then that prospects of such splendour were twenty years away.

Dorothy had an attractive way of narrowing her eyes and changing her respiration at the same time, thus looking at you – shrewdly. This pause and attitude was not her natural disposition.

She was not a calculating person, but certain changes in her personality could be credited only to great acting ability or unconscious imitation of other people.

Physically she was most attractive, and would have made a wonderful actress. Her figure was full, petite, curvaceous and voluptuous. She had an extraordinary, musical, carrying voice, which was her greatest charm. Many of the patients and staff were unreasonably jealous of her many fascinations, but I only regarded her as perfect and infallible, in her own sphere of course.

Her ugly sister visited her once a week. She brought lots of cream cakes, chocolates, cigarettes and a large flask of coffee each time. Dorothy and I shared the coffee when 'she' left. I was so lonely when she went back, three months later, to her stepmother. I cried frequently, and when I looked around I saw nothing but Picassos where there once was a Renoir.

Chapter 3

Six months in those early days seemed like six years at least. It was now summer in the admission. For a week now I had slept out on the glass-topped verandah. Selected patients, whom the staff trusted, were allowed to 'sleep out'. It was cool out there, but my thoughts were far from cool that hot summer.

I had spent the day chopping thistles outside the admission block. As I chopped the beastly things, a plan formed in my mind, to escape from the Big House that night. I hid my clothes under my mattress. Just before dawn, I dressed quietly behind the verandah, ran across the field and climbed over a wall. I managed the wall easily, as I was only twenty then and very agile. The sun was just lighting the sky when I walked hastily down to the town, a short distance away. I was fuming inwardly at what I thought was my long unnecessary confinement. I was fleeing in my own mind from a thousand demons.

The staff found me thirty minutes later in a telephone kiosk. I was taken back, in ignominy, by car. Years later, I met again one of the four nurses who had been with me in the car, and asked her to whom I had been telephoning. She told me sincerely and honestly, that I had phoned 999 and then I had asked for Whitehall 1212. The perplexed telephone operator had passed on the information to the Big House. Today I can hardly believe that I could do such an irrational thing, but when one is twenty, the greatest nonsense is acceptable as gospel; one plays the lone wolf and one is forced back to the herd for lack of other wolves.

On my return, I was immediately put to bed in the observation

ward, disgraced, and the subject of much conjecture among the
newly admitted patients. I was angry with myself for the failure of
my desperate solo flight to freedom. I was a marked woman now,
I thought in exasperation! I would be considered 'unstable'.

My mother arrived three days after my attempted escape. She
arrived unheralded and obviously all in a flutter. Her shocked
voice told me she disapproved, and I knew, as I knew her, that it
was something she had not foreseen.

When the recriminations were over I said: 'Was there anything
in the paper about it?'

'Of course not, dear, but then I wrote a letter to the editor.'

'Ah!' I said, satisfied. I could imagine her immediate letter to
the editor of the local rag, urging his discretion in the non-
publication of such material, and, of course, she would subtly
remind him that his daughter and I had attended the same school.

'Now dear, listen to me, promise me you will never do that
again.'

'Mother, I want you to claim me out.'

'I have to see the doctor first, dear,' she said soothingly, and
then immediately plied me with questions as to what I ate and
how I slept. I explained patiently, yet a little irritably, that one
could not sleep under blazing arc lights all night unless one was
deaf and blind.

'Sedatives are given, and the sedatives are sleeping draughts
too, if you keep everybody else awake, or if you have chronic
insomnia.'

'Well, dear, you could switch off the lights . . .'

'This is not a nursing home, Mother. I happen to be in the
observation ward now, where all is light, morning, noon and . . .
do you know, Mother, there is a kind, gentle, beautiful nun in here
who could no longer bear the darkness of the great silence, and
she confided in me that Reverend Mother sent her in here because
she put on the lights at night in the convent at that sacred time.'

Mother digested this information, for her own pure fictional
records of course, for future reference. If her account to her friends
of the Big House seemed too 'racy' at times, she would subtly
weave into her original account this pathos of a lonely light-loving

martyr, longing for companionship, peace, normality and light, yet deterred by a medieval, rigid, inflexible rule. My mother and her friends had the highest respect for religious, and this might indicate how fatalistic for everyone, including myself, our sojourn was in this dark, unpredictable world. This pain-deadening morphia I unconsciously meted out, occasionally, out of a sense of pity, which was more self-destructive than wise. Had I been wiser then, I should have kept silence, which, I noticed as the years went on, spurred relatives to take the initiative, and for ever end the boring and inconvenient visits.

Mother took an orange from the bag on my locker and began to peel it for me.

'Now, dear, tell me, dear, who were you phoning to in Whitehall 1212? I heard it all,' she said significantly.

Truthfully I said: 'Scotland Yard I think. I thought they might send a secret agent to rescue me.' I lowered my voice to a conspiratorial whisper. 'Mother,' I said, 'they are needed very badly here, there is something very sinister going on . . .'

She looked at me as if suddenly I had become a changeling, and said out loud, for the benefit of a nurse passing by, 'Now dear, the nurses are your friends, you are to get well.'

She smiled charmingly again at a nurse who glided by with pursed lips, discreet demeanour, behaving as if she was a fairy princess in a world of gnomes, ghouls and changelings. Oh well, I thought, so that's the game. Mother openly approved of my gaolers, and I must kow-tow to all and sundry. I consoled myself with the thought that once Mother's protective, defensive streak is aroused, beware the Big House, for there would be some manipulating and duping in higher circles. These people, she had often assured me, were criteria of predictable behaviour. I smiled wryly, remembering that Mother also thought nobody was a free agent, but that all were susceptible to romantic formulae and inducements. She lived sublimely, from day to day, solving each particular problem she was confronted with daily, and amazed that the next problem should come so soon after.

'Sufficient for the day . . .'

I finished the orange, and as Mother took up her handbag and

shopping bag, I felt suddenly afraid, afraid of her apparent ignorance of the mental hell that I was in, of her seeming indifference
to her departure, now imminent. Loneliness, bitter lonely tenderness for her, surged inside me, which I could not now show, as she
was smiling bravely, and kissing me on my bed-damp cheek, with
that rare butterfly touch she reserved especially for me.

I hated myself then for failing her. She had expected so much
of me. I had resigned because of her really. How could I work
healing others, to put it sublimely, how could I work, far across
the sea, while she was all alone, struggling against the grain. Now,
she had to explain to her friends, invent and keep up appearances.
I choked out goodbye somehow – and returned her kiss, and suddenly I knew she had forgiven me. I, also, in my childish,
impulsive way, had gone against the grain, like an empty, wind-
tossed kite.

'Treatment' was meted out: salts in the morning, sedatives for the
restless in the day, and the inevitable liquid paraffin in the evening.
I was very bored, until the night a new and terrifying treatment
began, electroconvulsive therapy. From the first day it commenced
it was referred to in its abbreviated form – ECT. It was in its exper-
imental stage then. Patients went in 'live'; now I believe they are
given injections first, to render them unconscious.

It began very dramatically. The doors into and out of the wards
were locked, except for the door leading into the middle dormitory.
Three beds stood ready inside, isolated in the centre of the small
dormitory. Two small tables were behind the first bed. The beds
were specially prepared, the top bed clothes were tidy, and there
were little post-operative packets at the foot of each bottom-sheeted
bed. Screens were placed around the beds, thus making a private
little ECT operating theatre. Bowls of swabs, sterile drums, forceps,
saline, the lot, were hastily brought in and put on one of the tables.
There was a white cloth on the table, as it was lacquered and slip-
pery. Six extra nurses arrived, and finally the psychiatrist, carrying
by the handle his little 'black box'. One patient, who seems
obsessed with this treatment, calls it 'the magic apparatus' with such
reverence, or superstition, that it leaves doubt as to her sanity.

At 8pm the 'music' began. During the trial period of ECT three patients were 'done' each night, Sundays excepted. Who the patients were, or where they came from, I do not know, but my eyes observed fearfully, and I quaked beneath my bedclothes, which I clutched tightly up to my chin. The patients were half dragged, half propelled, one by one, to the ECT inside.

They kicked and screamed, without exception, and one patient lay on the floor and was dragged in. The reassuring voice of the psychiatrist could be heard, in between certain ejaculatory protests:

'No, now, Jane, shush, it will all be over in a minute.'

Sometimes an unpleasant scuffle could be heard and the psychiatrist would say in command: 'Hold her, nurse.'

Once he, or they, rather, succeed in getting the apparatus on, the unwilling victim is under control. A cool swab of saline is then splashed on to the temples of the patient, then the ECT apparatus is strapped around her head, and buckled in front on the forehead. He then puts on some other apparatus himself, fiddles cleverly with his little electric box, considers – zero – out for the count – the patient.

The bed with the still, quiet body of the patient is wheeled outside the screens, and a satisfied murmuring command is heard: 'Next, nurse.'

Another protesting, witch-ridden poor soul is then forced down the aisles, through the door, to the monster's den.

To complete, three now unconscious bodies sleep side by side or in a row. A few minutes later, while the screens are removed and the mopping-up exercise begins, the psychiatrist emerges, smiling, which ought to instil confidence in us. He goes to the wash-basin, opposite me, performs his ablutions vigorously, and sometimes pensively. He then jauntily departs with his little black box.

Although many patients had twenty or thirty shots of ECT, their behaviour conformed always to the above pattern – terror, violent resistance, and dreaded anticipation.

Chapter 4

Breakfast was at 9am. There was a plate of porridge for everyone, with plenty of powdered milk. Fresh milk was given as 'extras' at appropriate times between meals. The second and last course for breakfast was one thick buttered slice of bread and butter, and on Sundays, when porridge was not served, there were two thick large slices of bread and butter. To wash it down were churns of boiled tea, milked and sugared before transport by the motor van from the general kitchen to the ward kitchens. If the van broke down, a horse and cart did the job with no undue haste, in which case breakfast was late and the tea was spoiled of course. I was mainly interested in the porridge. The powdered milk spoiled it, I thought, so I endeavoured to change it into a kind of chocolate pudding by mixing a tin of condensed milk with cocoa and mixing all through my porridge. That was before I lost my appetite, of course.

'Extras' were left to the discretion of the charge nurse, who considered delicacy, old age, and medical reasons her priorities in this matter. If a new patient wanted an egg or a glass of milk each day, she was obliged to ask a psychiatrist, who would then instruct the nurse to put her on the list for 'extras'.

Lunch was served at tables in the dining rooms, or day-rooms. In rotation there was corned beef and cabbage – it was the only vegetable the hospital grew – and potatoes, boiled mutton or boiled beef. Everything was boiled, as there had to be soup. Half a mug of soup was given daily with the meat and vegetables. The liquid in which the meat had cooked was the soup. No bread was served at lunch if potatoes were served. For three months every

15

year we had one huge slice of dry bread instead of potatoes, which were usually going bad two months before the substitution. There was undressed boiled whiting on Fridays, and it was completely tasteless. To follow, tapioca – cooked probably in watery milk, as it had that translucent glow – was served. Water was served on demand, but water glasses were not allowed, and the mugs were wanted for the soup and tea. Of course, it's all changed now, and unbreakable cups were used before I left.

In between the three meals, patients longed for exotic foods, anything their friends took them in, or anything in the confectionery line which they could purchase in the little hospital tuck shop. Tea was given to the bed patients after lunch, on a trolley. Patients who worked had their tea in the sewing rooms and the laundry at 11am and 3.30pm. This tea and bread and butter and jam was a reward for the work and the only pay received.

Supper was at six in winter and seven in summer. It was always the same: two 'doorsteps' of bread and butter with boiled tea. Most of us were so hungry that we swallowed it thankfully without a murmur. Extras were passed around for people who had food from visitors, for pensioners who were given extras from the shop, and, of course, the Big House extra, for the privileged – the evening or morning egg. Hot or warm milk was given to very old or ill patients last thing at night, to help them sleep, patients whose only insanity appeared to be apathy or despair or bewilderment at the strange communal life they found themselves in.

There was one such little woman. She never spoke, she never complained. She walked up and down all day, and she would not sit unless she was actually made to. She walked rather like a fast robot, with a type of goose-step, her arms usually folded on her breast. As she walked, her eyes, like gimlets, would scan every inch of the floor, and she interrupted her steady gait only to stop and pick up unknown objects. Once, with horror, I saw it was a lighted cigarette end. She put it into her mouth, as a fish takes a fly, and continued on her route, arms folded, jaw moving imperceptibly from the chew. In gesture, in appeal, everything about her was pitiful, pathetic, and yet she was one of the unapproachable ones. She was as frail as a piece of Dresden china, and yet she wore the notorious criss-crossed jacket, which, next to the strait-jacket, is relatively indestructible.

I lost my appetite once or twice, because of worry and apprehension – the long detention, which was never explained to me, how long I would have to stay, what really had they deduced or observed. I was so preoccupied with the suspense that I lost all interest in food until I went to work, in the sewing room for a time, and finally in the laundry. Then, I always felt hungry. I trained myself in later years to eat for body fuel or calories. Sometimes, if I arrived early to the laundry, I would get a large helping of brown sausages from the kitchen, which was adjacent.

The cutlery was terrible. The knives, stainless steel, were too big, too heavy and too blunt and tiring to use. The dessert spoons were only light cutlery. The forks, like the knives, were just a heavy length of iron or steel, with the minimum serration for gripping with. A count check for security was done after all meals. No patient could leave her table until all the cutlery was counted, checked and double checked, after which the cutlery was washed and locked away by the nurses responsible. In these searches I never once saw them succeed in finding anything on any person there. Sometimes the missing cutlery was found in the waste bucket and sometimes outside, thrown out by a secretive, irrational, sometimes irritable patient.

If you did not eat, it was said to you in no uncertain terms that you were deteriorating. All these minor trivialities of taste and distaste were translated into obscure technical terms and put as obstacles to release on enquiries from relatives.

I went off the food. Mother arrived unexpectedly to visit me. I looked up and saw Mother, smiling, pathetic, courageous. 'What's this, dear, I hear about your not eating? You know you have to eat.'

'Mother, appetite is not everything. I shall eat when I go home. The food is rather monotonous.'

She opened the shopping bag on her knee.

'Look, dear, some of your favourites – oranges, cake, chocolate.'

I accepted them silently, then I said: 'Have you been to see the superintendent? When can I go home?'

Mother looked sadly at me.

'He wants you to have the insulin shock treatment, dear, and I have to sign a form today agreeing, as you are not twenty-one.'

Horrified, I said: 'Mother, I don't need any treatment, honestly I don't. I am not happy here, that's all. I will be all right when I go home. Was it because I tried to escape, was it?'

She lowered her eyes.

'Well, partly, dear, but you see this shock treatment will increase your appetite and make you well again.'

I felt a sinking in my stomach. Mother, I could discern, was committed to signing the form.

'It is the only thing I can do now, dear. The psychiatrist says it will be very beneficial for you.'

'Beneficial!' I said shrilly, 'I don't want their benefits. Let some poor person who really needs it have it. I don't. Insulin treatment takes three whole months. That is the usual time for the course, including recuperation. Mother, please don't sign!'

She patted and stroked my hand.

'It will be nothing, dear, I will come in to see you in a few weeks.'

I was stunned. I had no say in my own life.

'Who is that lady next to your bed, dear?'

This I knew was a sudden question on Mother's part simply to cause a diversion, for her to recover her composure. She looked down at her through a chink in the curtains.

'She looks a sweet person.'

'Yes, Mother, and there she is, in here, guiltless, and yet the man who raped her in the chicken shed of her own farm gets off scot-free. It is he who should be put in, not her.'

I did not describe how shamed and humiliated she had been, how the man was exempted from blame, how she had told me her emotions, to explain why she had agreed with her sisters, afterwards, to come into the Big House to hide away, for they declined to publicise the scandal.

Mother fondled her chamois gloves.

'That's it, dear. The woman always pays. That's life.'

My greeny-blue eyes questioned her assumption, and to my annoyance, she changed the subject.

'I shall have to sign permission for the treatment on my way out, when I see the doctor,' she reminded me.

'The experiment, you mean,' I said bitterly.

As Mother kissed me goodbye I relented a little.

'Please write and let me know the result. He might change his mind.'

I fervently prayed it might be so.

Chapter 5

It was not to be so. The next morning I was told to fast – no break-fast. I had no idea the first day that it would sicken me. Patients who had had it told me they felt nothing, just a prick of the needle and then they awoke to find themselves drinking a bowl of glucose.

I was injected with insulin early in the morning. I came around from my unconscious or perhaps semi-unconscious state always experiencing the same sensation. I felt dizzy, I saw tiny blue circles or lights, and I would suddenly find myself struggling, trying to overcome the colour, the sensation of dizziness, and then I would find myself weakly obeying a voice which said:

'Drink this down now, it will make you all right.'

I would become conscious then of a huge mug of shiny white liquid stickiness pressed to my lips. I would gulp it down, until the reaction, and then I would retch violently. I felt exhausted, weak, ill, and I was disgusted with such a sickening treatment.

I had had three mornings of this treatment when I was told my mother had arrived to visit me. Naturally, she was full of loving solicitude, and she asked me how I felt after the treatment, if it agreed with me. At this question I was whipped, sick in thought and stomach.

'Haven't they told you?' I said weakly.

'No, dear.' She looked surprised.

I feebly explained, almost getting sick again at the memory. She sympathised, and said she would see the doctor herself and explain. She tempted me then with the extras, fussing over me, breaking the peeled orange into segments, eating one piece herself. Although I felt ill, I took some of the dainties, firmly insisting, though, that the treatment was wholly unsuitable for me. A peaceful silence enveloped us, a thoughtful mental conflict of opinions, unexpressed.

A voice broke the silence and the spell. It was the voice of a newly admitted patient, audible through the screens nearby. 'Well, Maud my dear, that poor girl behind the screens, they are giving her insulin, and I heard . . . you know where they get it? Well I heard it is pig's insulin. Fancy putting pig's muck into human beings!'

There was a sudden intake of Mother's breath. 'Really, Honor, there is no privacy here.' She looked angry. 'Don't worry, dear, I'll see the doctor and find out all about it.'

'Mother, please don't bother about the insulin, I know it's from pigs, just explain that I can't keep the glucose down.' Mother departed, not so confidently as usual, to her session with the psychiatrist.

The treatment continued for the next week, Sunday excepted. The psychiatrist was not easily discouraged from his experiments, and he explained to me, tersely, that naturally it was revolting to me, but that I should persevere, that the course was two-thirds over, and it would be recorded for posterity in the hospital archives.

'However,' he said, 'I have been speaking to your mother, and she is going to take you up fruit squash to put through the glucose.' He patted my head in a fatherly way. 'It won't be so bad then, will it, my dear?'

I wanted to say that I was not his 'dear' and that only a sadistic monster would deliberately sicken me, day after day, in some mad experiment between me and a pig's extract. I had three more days of this particular ordeal, when I was told by a nurse that I should cheer up now, as there was only one week more of 'insulin shock' and then I would be finished with it. I was mentally digesting this information when Mother arrived unexpectedly, three days earlier than usual.

I was delighted to see her and miserably I again complained of the vile treatment. She opened her bag and took out a bottle of lime squash and a bottle of orange squash and told me to give them to the nurses later. She had arranged it all with the doctor, she told me, triumphantly.

I enquired about people at home, and if she herself was happy, and so forth. To my relief, she told me that she had never had so many friends calling, or so many invitations. Everybody, it seemed, wanted to hear of my progress, and Mother had a great time inventing her own version of the Big House and of her now familiar knowledge of psychiatry. One of the committee members had called and offered her a lift up to see me. That was the reason she had come, she explained.

She remained for about an hour. As she bent over to kiss me goodbye, she said: 'If there is anything you want, dear, please write and I will take it up.' She left, and I remarked she seemed happier somehow. I called the nurse and offered her the bottle of squash.

'I wonder now,' I thought, 'what will the fruit juice do to the glucose?'

The next morning I knew. It made it easier to vomit. I got rid of the glucose faster, and without the sickening retching. And it made the sweet, sickly taste of the glucose less nauseating.

The reports of my constant reaction to the treatment must have been believed at last, for, two days before Mother arrived again, I was told that the treatment was over and I could get up.

This period after my insulin treatment I consider a signpost or a crucial period in my life. I was no longer a bed patient in the observation ward. I worked a little, wrote letters, and I expected to be sent home after the next monthly 'inspection'. Each month, the exact date varying, male and female patients were selected and called to attend the super's office for 'inspection'. This was a general term and did not mean what it implied. The super and two staff psychiatrists interviewed each selected patient separately. Half only of the meagre few selected passed this 'inspection' or inter-view. No patient, however deserving, could be 'called up' for this 'inspection' either, unless his or her relatives had sent in a letter beforehand claiming out the patient. If the letter was sent but arrived too late, the patient's liberty was automatically deferred to the next month's board business.

When the date for inspection became known, gossip circulated, back and forth, as to what the lucky names were. It might be the doctor – he would perhaps drop a hint casually, advising a patient to write home for a letter of application, and he might suggest that if it arrived in time the chances of release were very good. The legal machinery was then in motion, and it only remained for the board to endorse it. Many 'inspected' patients failed to qualify for release and were asked to wait longer. The psychiatrist would suggest a little more rest, or, perhaps, a little more treatment. Those who failed became abject and miserable, as, often, they saw themselves as free, even before they were 'inspected.'

Out of three thousand patients, only ten patients, on average, were discharged each month. The exodus was always equalled if not exceeded by the influx. As time went on, many patients who were ready to be discharged became permanent inmates because the requisite letter of application was not sent in. People made excuses, there were other pressing cares outside, and the patient became 'the last straw' to the caretaker government – the families outside. The patients inside, expectant, waited for the letters and the visits, until finally, one day, they would find themselves rejects, outcasts, and no explanation given. Sometimes a crushed spirit breaks, from mental agony and anguish, when she understands at last that she is a captive in a free society.

Patients at first struggle violently against this unexplained veto on their human rights. In their secret being, dignity and hopelessness clasp, to emerge vacantly, as inscrutable amnesia, or, sometimes, as an unknown actor or actress, a weeping or a laughing clown. Tears and laughter in such conditions are true, yet unrelated often to the primeval instincts experienced . There is an obvious emotional numbness, but it is often a mask or a disguise, assumed, that precludes questioning. One becomes aware of all the defence mechanisms, the pathetic remains, of human dignity. To the stranger they appear odd, aloof, unfriendly and unapproachable. To the initiated, their eccentric behaviour merely demonstrates, in many guises, their own pent-up emotions and disappointments. Some unwanted patients, in their aloneness, act as if they are the sole representatives of a family somehow spirited away by occult means. They reminisce, and remark family resemblances in other patients, and a friendship develops, of substitution. Two such patients often walk arm-in-arm, talk nonsense, to have nonsense returned, and prove an old adage – friends in need are friends indeed.

Chapter 6

I expected mother to claim me out any day now. Treatment was over, and there were signs I was going, little things like my return to the inner dormitory, where the lights were put out at night. I had now a certain amount of sleep, although the two-hourly visits of the night nurse, who switched on the lights each time, alerted me, and often I could not get back to sleep.

I worked at different chores. I was indifferent, almost, to my surroundings. I longed for Mother's next visit and, I thought, my subsequent freedom. I even played a prank with some of the 'wild ones' on a patient who tried all our patience. She, for reasons, or no reasons, of her own, dashed each night straight down to bed, to be first there. When we, the majority, arrived, she was usually in another patient's bed, leaving her own vacant. She thought it a great joke to go into a different bed each night, and to be the centre of attention when the rightful occupant arrived. In desperation, I suggested to the 'wild set' that we should make her 'bed conscious'. One of us would go down early before supper, put one of the neatly rolled floor rugs in a bolster cover and leave it in her bed, to suggest it was occupied.

I had been selected to 'prepare' her when supper was over.

'Josie, I want you,' I said.

'Yes, what is it? I have to go to my bed.'

'You don't have to go just yet, Josie. Anyhow, there is someone in your bed.'

'My bed! Impossible, I'm always there first.'

'Well, come and see.'

We all followed her as she hastened to her bed, and, certainly, a long figure was outlined, bed clothes over head, apparently.

She shook the rug, then she pulled back the clothes and realised what it was. She accused us all of interfering with her bed. We denied all responsibility. The plan inexplicably worked, for she never again forgot her own bed.

I was feeling more cheerful each day, and at last the day arrived for Mother's visit. She came towards me. I could see her face was unusually pale, and that she had been weeping. Her usually gentle pale blue eyes were sombre, and all dark iris. She said nothing at first, just a long, heart-rending look, then she whispered, in a pathetic, lovable, childish way: 'Honor, Fred, he's gone.'

Tiny little dewdrop tears rolled down her cheeks.

'Gone? Fred?' I repeated.

I spoke quietly, slowly, and with a sinking heart. I knew what she was about to say – Fred, her dearest friend, had died.

Almost roughly, she put her damp handkerchief in her pocket, it had given her away, as if I did not know all the tears she must have cried before these.

'Yes, Honor, he is dead. He was in hospital for just three days. Pneumonia, Double, I think. He could not be moved, and there were complications . . .'

'Oh Mother,' was all I could say. What could I say? I felt so sorry for her, I knew she must feel far lonelier than I was.

I loved him too, the third cousin, the loyal, ever faithful, unpaid servant, the substitute father who adored me from baby-hood. My father died when I was five. The quiet man remained, Fred, the only saint in the house, the impoverished celibate, the lover of children, who gave all of his simple love and life to us, all without complaint. He loved Mother as he would a lovable, endearing, wayward child. Paul and I were his children, and I, house-bound, was his favourite, while Mother, well, only they alone knew what they meant to each other.

'Mother, I could go home with you, you must be very lonely. I am due for discharge anyhow.'

Mother looked at me miserably.

'No dear. I have seen the superintendent and I explained that your aunt has invited me to stay with her for a while, just a short holiday, dear, until I get over the shock, she says. Here, dear, some nice extras for you.'

She smiled sadly and passed some paper bags to me. I ate something, not knowing or caring if it were sawdust. 'You do look well, dear. It must be the insulin.'

'Damn the insulin. Oh I'm sorry, Mother. It hasn't made any difference, you know. I'm still the same naughty Honor.'

I smiled, although I felt sad and wretched. I felt like a buffoon, saying the wrong words in the wrong scene. My whole world was turning upside down. I spoke of how good the chocolate and orange tasted, anything to appear calm and normal, and not distress her further.

'You are not to worry about me, Mother, take a good long rest with Aunty.'

Then she cried again, a few more uncontrollable tears. Tears were all she had, apart from the widow's mite. She gave all generously – tears, love and the mite. My own heart at that moment felt strange, as if it were drip-drying, wrung out in its own saline solution. I vainly tried to quiet it, soothe it, but Mother sensed the clamour, the savage pathos imprisoned within. I was unable to help her, to bring back the dead. No, but if I could, strange, I thought, it is my father I would bring back to her. That was the only time she was really happy. I knew this from her diary, which she had dedicated to me the year of my birth.

She leaned over and kissed my forehead.

'Poor darling. I will be back soon. The doctor knows I can't take you home now, just yet.'

When Mother had gone I reviewed the problem. I felt she was, in a way, worse off than I was. Her best friend dead, Paul away, under some strain, I suppose, while I, whom she loved, was now only a reproach to her. Daughter, presumably, has nervous breakdown, not really, just depression, nothing serious; Mother goes on holiday, following bereavement, and when she returns from kind Aunty, she will then take daughter home. Oh it was so simple, and according to the general rules or principles of life, it should be – a simple expectation of the obvious. Crisis was over, anti-climaxes were over, or almost over. There is no drama. Clown, get thee to a nunnery.

To nurses and patients I explained:

When Mother returns from her holiday . . .

Lena was friendly, and I confided my hopes to her, and she forgot Jeff for a few minutes to say:

'Poor kid, never mind, you won't feel the month passing. Keep your pecker up.'

I took this advice literally. I wanted no more hitches, so I ate the portion of food allotted to me daily, and, by hope and prayer, I kept the vision of liberty alive. A patient is ruled by the psychiatric monopoly, of which she knows nothing. She will do nothing right with them, for she, the patient, does not know the rules, but she learns, when it is too late, that there is no compromise, no explanation, given by the monopoly. They reason with you, but only when it is too late. When the rule is broken, when the damage is done, only then is the remedy applied. The vital statistics are waiting, the moments for truce, negotiation, pass as lamentable conceit. The opposition builds up its own rules, unaware of the simple precedent of the monopoly, which will not explain its own rules in simple terms of social relevance, and ending up denouncing all others. Other places, also, as the Big House, prepare graphically for the everlasting siege, and stir dolorously the 'bird's nest soup'.

The bath nurse's voice came towards me, as from a great distance.

'Will you be bathed now, Honor?'

'Bathed,' I repeated vaguely. 'Oh yes, nurse, I will be there in a minute.'

I undressed and joined the queue for baths and 'weighing in'. I clutched my bath towel around my naked body fiercely, not daring to speak to anyone. I would be a query now. I could imagine the voices . . .

I thought Honor was going home . . .

Won't they take her out?

This would go on and on until my home and person became a legend.

The bath brought me back to the present, or the past. It didn't really matter, present or past. I could say, there is nobody to contradict me, time begins with this bath, or in this queue. I have just about as much interest now in time as the sea has in the obliging rivers.

I go in at last, I must have waited an hour, but that is unreal here, I will say I waited fifteen-queue-deep-time, more appropriate. I am weighed and it is written down. I step up to the ghastly 'bath' unit. I wait for the half-cold douche of washing soda and soapy water, poured down on me from a huge swan-like enamel jug, with routine detachment. It stings my upturned screwed-up face. I close my eyes tighter, and bow my head, and hold it steady as it is lathered. The soap cloths are applied vigorously. Another jug of rinsing water is poured over me, and I step out again, from the devil-invented soda fountain, too miserable to recollect what I had decided to think about, and too tired to care. I wanted to go to the dormitory, to the darkness, to think, to come to terms with, almost, another ghoulish nightmare. It was still three more hours to bedtime, when I could go and hide myself, pretend I was asleep, and evade the questions, and the overpowering righteousness of the compromising multitude. A pity we could not all unite and conquer the common demon, but just now we could be compared to disciplined mercenaries, or rebellious guerrillas, not sure of their camouflage. It all depended on your allies.

Chapter 7

Six weeks from the date of her last visit, I received a note saying Mother would visit me at the usual time. It was just then I realised she had to return to that large, dismal house after her holiday, to an unaired bed, damp, wet walls, and chilly, ghostly memories of the sweet, sad days that had flitted by, as a swift cloud passing before a wan moon. She would not care, I knew, about those hazards to her health. She would be oblivious of the discomforts, and suffer all with her usual patience. She would miss Fred especially.

I was delighted to see her again, plenty of pink in her cheeks, all amusing anecdotes about Aunty's dry wit and John's humour. They were like Darby and Joan, according to Mother. She was so loving, so delighted to see me, bringing me little gifts, and some even from Aunty. When she was leaving, I reminded her to send in the application for the coming month, and she said she would. I would get a job at home, and live with her. I went back to the hated ward, joy in my heart, knowing that it was now only a matter of three weeks until I was free again. I had been a hospital probationer in a hospital in London, during the Blitz, but that was nothing compared to this whirlpool. I said I never wanted to see another hospital again. The unnatural sterile element in it almost sickened me. Eight years later, I remember I compared myself to a shanghaied citizen. I could never believe I had struggled through all my childhood of illnesses, measles, chickenpox, that I had studied to pass the matriculation in eight subjects, to be told obliquely that I was ineffectual, to become a byword, or even worse, to be remembered as a sort of female village idiot. The superintendent, I anticipated, would consider Mother's formal application, the obvious course, and agree to my release. It was very simple really. 'Beloved daughter taken home by mother.'

It was not to be.

Mother arrived, looking very business-like, on her next visit, and greeted me with her usual love and tenderness, handing me the usual paper bags.

'Some little extras for you, dear.'

We were now in a small waiting-room specially reserved for visitors. Mother, of course, was not aware of our privilege – being left alone. She nibbled a chocolate meditatively.

'Well, dear, here I am again.'

'I am so glad to see you, Mother. I'm all excited at the thought of leaving. Have you written, the letter, you know, the application, because . . .'

The chocolate eaten, Mother turned all her attention to me.

'Well dear, that is what I want to talk to you about. Money is very scarce. I have taken in two paying guests.'

'But Mother, what have they got to do with my going home? We have another spare room, haven't we?'

'Well, no dear, not exactly. I have rented the spare room to a seamstress, and they will want my bedroom; they share, you see, the bedroom beside the sitting room. They will want to use the sitting room, but of course, I will use it also, dear,' Mother said hastily, seeing my look of absolute bewilderment. 'I will have to sleep in your room myself, Honor.'

I gasped audibly. No room in my own home! A premonition of impending disaster came upon me. Surely not, I thought, not again, not now, when I can go with their blessing. My joy was totally eclipsed, and a dull ache inhabited my dawning suspicions.

'What does that matter? I can share with you, Mother.'

I laughed, although my immediate reaction was fear, fear that my precious liberty was in jeopardy. I tried to understand the implications of her words, but failed. I had never imagined such a possibility, ever.

'Don't you want to know who they are, dear?'

'I don't care. Who are they?' I answered again in a dull, flat, voice.

'Well you remember Miss Moore and Miss Blissim, your French and history teachers . . . well, dear, they heard about your little depression . . . and they called to enquire after you. We had quite a few chats, and they decided to come and stay with me, for company, you know. They had a miserable time in that cold, cheerless hotel, you know the one dear, near the delicatessen. They asked me if I would take them as paying guests, until you are well enough to come home. They said, now that Fred is gone, and I am all alone, and your brother Paul is away permanently, working, they would try to cheer me up. It was kind of them, dear, and I do so need the money. They are moving in their luggage today, while I am here with you.'

There was still a faint hope left.

'Oh well, Mother, of course, if you need the money, that's all right with me. It was kind of them. I can share your, our, room. You say it is only temporary.'

'It is so difficult to explain, dear. I know how disappointed you will be, having to wait a little longer. Honor, to tell you the truth, I haven't been feeling well lately.'

I gave a little gasp of anguish and disappointment, all mixed up together.

'Mother, what will I do now? The doctor said I may go as soon as you send in the application. I was all ready to go, it's not fair. I shan't stay here. It's hell, really it is, Mother.'

'You would not want me to have a relapse now, dear, you might lose sleep, and appetite and worry about me.'

I broke in beseechingly.

'Oh! no! please, Mother, don't.'

A vision passed before my eyes for a moment, of my poor mother's scars, hidden, but to my eyes a cruel, horrible desecration by sadistic surgeons.

'Please, Mother, you can't say such a thing. I assure you I would be far happier and well at home with you, no matter what the inconveniences, than in this horrible place. What did the superintendent say?'

'He . . .' Mother slowly said 'thought . . . that . . . in these circumstances . . . my health especially, dear, that . . . as I was unprepared . . . to take you out . . . that he could not discharge you . . . just yet.'

My brain reeled under the impact of this unforeseen obstacle. I had thought the way was clear, and now it had to be my own sweet, lovable mother who unwittingly lashed me with her every sentence, stung me almost to undaughterly retorts of reproach and reproof. Somehow I just could not reproach her, at least not without deference to her authority. I was the only one she had authority over now, and I could not hurt her now by accusing her of cruelty she was unaware of.

'It's not that I am complaining of my health, dear, but Doctor Hazel says if my condition disimproves further, I may have to go into hospital myself. I think I must have caught a cold in my kidneys again, and now he says I may have to take tablets for my heart.'

I thought, the damp house, I might have known, but her heart . . . her sacrificial heart, that I had benefited so often from. I could not believe my ears. Up to this, I had always hated the beastly surgeons who had lacerated her body, and now – who could I hate, or what.

I surrendered. I sighed, resignedly. This problem which now confronted me was such that it was best not to think of it, because my own selfish wishes were inextricable.

'Then what shall I say to the staff, the patients, that you cannot take me home just yet?' I asked, though almost petrified.

'Yes, dear, try and be patient, everything will turn out all right now, don't worry.'

In a daze, I watched her prepare to go.

'Honor, dear, you will write, and I will come up once a week as usual.'

I saw my nurse come in, one of my keepers now.

'Yes of course, Mother,' I said mechanically. 'The little outing will do you good.'

Mother stood up stiffly.

'I have to go now, dear. Honor, I hope you are not too disappointed. Poor Fred, I miss him. Do you, Honor?'

'Yes indeed, more than I can say. If he were alive, he would ask you to take me out. He would not leave me in here one minute. I was his daughter, at least he loved me as if I were.'

I stopped, the dam was giving way, the long pent-up flood of tears was welling and rising in my heart. In just a matter of seconds, they would arrive at the great lakes of my eyes, and I would collapse, emotionally, with sheer misery and loneliness and pity. I compressed my lips as tightly as I could, and kissed Mother goodbye, quickly, briskly almost, in my desire to conceal from her the salty dew that was seeping out through my eyes.

'Goodbye dear, remember it's not your fault, be good, don't give any cause for complaint.'

She was gone. I cried desolately. I returned to the day-room. I sat on a chair, against a window, and looked out dejectedly. I thought of the twist of fate that was getting me more entangled every day. I was in the hands of fate, which, like the river, flows at its own sweet will. Mentally, beaver-like, I looked for something to dam it, looking around, shaggily, for props, anything, to hold up the unheeding gush, and make again a cool limpid pool of quiet, hopeful, ordered thought for myself. I imagined the cool calm water caressing my head, smoothing wetly my fiery thatch. I longed for the limpid caressing water, lapping around my immersed body with head just above, waiting for the hot tears in my head to cool, and slow, to the body heat of the secure pool, the new environment I had made – imagined.

Chapter 8

After many nights of intense self-analysis, and analysis of Mother's actions and complex motives, I gave up. I could see no immediate solution anyhow. I felt tired and weary of my own indignation, and thinking about the possibilities of Mother's illness saddened me. Thought led me around in circles, and back again to the beginning.

I suddenly wanted a Bible, and I had not got one. I tried to remember the reasons and explanations given in it for our existence. I wrote into a notebook I had with me among my scanty possessions all I could remember of the creation and Christian thought. I wrote simply, detaching myself from my own conflicts. I felt better after I re-read it, although it left much to be desired for orthodoxy. Still, it helped me to escape temporarily from my own thoughts, and I pondered which of the two worlds was the most difficult to comprehend – the old world of banishment and penalisation over an apparently trivial piece of fruit, or my world of the present, where there is banishment by proxy, or some other cunning, cumulative trivia.

I went more often to church; it was peaceful there, and sheltered. The stained-glass windows were heavenly and I forgot temporarily, while there, the uncurtained windows of the underprivileged. The males are on one side and the females on the other. They wait for the little bell to ring. All is subdued, respectful, recollection. Some kneel and pray, some sit and merely stare ahead, their cares temporarily forgotten. Old Mother Hubbard, for example, an old lady from Sunset House – the 'last ditch'. I had visited there once or twice on messages with a nurse, so the old lady who usually sits in the centre of the chapel congregation, who fusses, who cannot settle herself to pray unless she fidgets with her drapery, is just a Mother Hubbard to me. With the humble and underprivileged are the privileged, worshipping side by side, the staff and the 'paroles'. The 'tobacco barons' are there, symbols of 'traffic', monopoly or favour. The long lanky man is always there, one of the 'distinguished' ones. His face is tired-looking yet calm, and a faint reminiscent smile always plays about his lips, lighting up his lean, clever face.

It was while I was attending those evening devotions in the chapel that the idea of another escape germinated in my mind. It was a late autumn evening, duskish, when I noticed the chaplain's car. He went inside the sacristy door as we arrived. I noticed he had locked neither the car nor the boot. It remained fixed in my mind that here was a means of escape.

I formed a plan. I would leave the back seat that I would occupy in the chapel, unobtrusively, and go outside quickly and, also as quickly, jump into the boot of the car. There I would lie doggo until I arrived at the bishop's palace, where the clergy and our chaplain resided. I would remain until it was dark, and then I would stealthily take leave of the palace grounds. There was just one obstacle to my freedom, which I thought about for hours before I solved the problem. I realised that if the boot door snapped and shut automatically as I secreted myself inside, I might suffocate, and thus defeat my purpose. I arrived at this solution, after much mental gymnastics: I would take with me a small twig, of a tree or a bush, and I would jam it in the boot hinge, so preventing it from locking, while at the same time allowing me just sufficient air to survive until nightfall.

I found a very suitable stick, after much searching on the walks. I concealed this in my toilet bag in the day, and transferred it to my pocket when I went to the chapel devotions in the evenings.

One evening – it had been a dark, gloomy day, and the sky threatened rain – I went to the devotions determined and prepared. I looked at the black thundery sky and I thought, happily, how dark it was, and propitious for my plan. The black shiny car was outside the chapel as usual. I knelt in the back seat in the chapel, and prayed that everything would go as planned. So far, so good. The nearest nurse was three seats away in front. There were three women on the aisle side of my seat. I moved to the end of the seat, to the gloomy side, noting that the women, who were obviously paroles, did not give me a glance. This move I made was strategic, for now I was in an unlighted, more obscure, place for my exit. I waited patiently. The paroles went out quickly. The congregation rose to sing the last hymn. I quickly left my seat for the shadows behind, and then I walked directly over to the door. It creaked as I opened it and I shivered at the noise, but the singing went on, and I was now outside in the porch. I closed the door quietly, and looked over at the shiny black car, just a few feet away.

'Now or never,' I said to myself, and, suiting the action to the words, I ran across to the boot. I had often seen people open a car boot, and no particular exertion was required, I understood. I pulled at the handle. It would not open for me. I panicked. I turned the handle desperately, and pulled again. Not one inch could I lift it. I pulled and pulled again. It was not locked, it couldn't be. I knew the chaplain had not done such a thing. I was certain.

I suddenly became aware of a deep silence behind me. The last hymn was sung, the devotions were over. I looked over my shoulder, my hands still pulling on the boot handle, and saw – the advance guard. Three nurses and three white coats were standing in the porch, looking over at me, then back to each other. Then they walked lazily towards me and closed in on my petrified ghost. I felt incorporeal, my legs felt as if they could no longer support me. Stupidly I took my hand off the boot handle, guilty, caught in the act. I was secretly chagrined. The senior nurse addressed me, peremptorily:

'What were you doing to the boot of the car?'

An unnecessary question, I thought.

Miss Probationer interrupted.

'I saw her, Nurse, she was trying to open the boot.'

'What for?' the third nurse asked in surprise.

'Honor, I shall have to report this,' said the senior nurse.

'What?' I said, innocently.

'Never you mind. Come on, girls, back.'

Symmetrically we crocodiled back. I managed on the way back to the admission to throw away the stick, unobserved. I guessed I had not heard the last of the episode, for I expected the incident to be reported, first of all to the charge nurse, then to the matron, finally ending up in my case-history, in the superintendent's files, unless – unless the nurses agreed among themselves that I was just idly testing the handle of the boot, in which case nothing would be reported. My prestige as a reliable character would be slightly impaired of course. As the hours passed, and I was not called for interrogation, I knew, in relief, that the episode was accepted as another involuntary, senseless, idiotic act. Although I was a potential escaper, they had no proof of my present intentions. They probably gave me credit for enough common sense not to suffocate myself. It's a funny thing, but if they had confronted me with the truth, I could not have denied it. If they said to me, in the 'court martial':

'So you do not deny it, you intended getting into the boot . . .' and they would pause, and exchange significant glances, '. . . to perhaps, suffocation. Is that it?'

And I would reply, unemotionally, 'Is that the only thing you accuse me of then, attempted suffocation?'

'You knew the hazards, total irresponsibility.'

I would then deal my master stroke, or mistress stroke, of self-defence:

'There was no hazard, there would be no suffocation.'

An incredulous, irritated 'Tch! Tch!' would be heard.

Then I would confound the lot, speaking slowly, distinctly, yet so modestly, so low, that the rhythmic 'tick-tock, tick-tock' of the court clock could plainly be heard as well:

'I had an airway with me, Sirs.'

Chapter 9

I sought refuge in religion after my narrow escape. The next day was not a day for devotions, so I took out my notebook digest of the Bible. Lena sat beside me, her knees to the wall, looking out of the window. A horse and rider galloped by the edge of the wood. Lena nodded her head in the direction of the rider, and said in a sarcastic drawl:

'Honor, those jodhpurs she's wearing, I wouldn't fancy them would you?'

I shoved the notebook in her direction, hurt at her lack of interest.

'They wouldn't suit you, Lena. A slinky evening gown and an ocelot is more in your line.'

She was pleased, and was just about to start in on Jeff, when I said, showing her the notebook: 'Lena, do you want to hear this or not?'

'Ye-ass, ye-ass,' she imitated the superintendent, and relaxed again in her chair.

I read on, unaware whether I had Lena's entire attention or not, but satisfied that at least I had a sympathetic listener. I expected some comments, naturally, on my uncensored efforts. When I relapsed into silence, Lena said, impatiently: 'That's all very fine, Honor, but they should have given more details.'

'I have been thinking, Lena, and I have a theory of my own. Supposing that the Bible spare ribs are really our floating ribs.'

Lena chuckled at a secret thought of her own. 'I didn't know my spare rib floated!'

'Well three do, Lena, in a manner of speaking,' I said.

'Is this your own concoction?'

'No, honestly. I studied anatomy when I did nursing.'

'I bet you did, Honor. Male or female?'

'Both,' I said, ruffled. 'All skeletons look alike; only a coroner would know the difference.'

Lena eyed me suspiciously.

'Honor, what do you read or think about? What good are theories? Marriage is the only theory I have part control of. The gilt is gone off the gingerbread, Honor. Jeff and my golden wedding that never existed.' She laughed hysterically, then calmed as quickly. 'You know what I mean, he's useless. When I see other married women with young lovely-looking husbands, kids, you know . . . Honor, when you marry, pick a dynamic individual, not a squib like I did.'

'Now, Lena, it can't be as bad as all that,' I said soothingly. 'Now, you've put me off, where was I?'

'You were at the "floating ribs".'

'Well, floating or sleeping, that's equivocal.'

'What's that?' asked Lena.

'Just a word I used, for brevity's sake.'

'That's right, play the sphinx, be brief, go ahead, but don't expect me to follow you.'

Lena looked around. Two nurses had come in, returning from their four o'clock tea. For their benefit, Lena said very loudly: 'It will soon be time for afternoon tea, darling, do go on with that dr-dreadful story.'

'Supposing – no interruptions please.' I looked reproachfully at the grim smile just coming on her lips.

'Go ahead, I might as well listen,' she said with tolerant amusement.

I began again.

'Adam had the use of his spare or floating ribs before God deadened them. They might even have been connected to the spine, as the other ribs now are, or maybe they were ribs but unconnected, with a special function or functions. If the original Adam was perfect, say, universally mobile, transient, superior to everything, might it not have been because of those spare or floating ribs? Why? Because they must have had a superior function.'

'My God, child, if you go on like this you might really go mad!'

I hastily reassured her. I knew she understood all right. She deliberately pretended to be dense on occasions.

'No, Lena, it is just a neat little theory I have packaged up. I can either credit it or discredit it. It is not a belief, just an idea.'

'It is a very long one,' said Lena, 'tell it to me in a nutshell.'

'I am trying to. Be patient. Now, have you ever noticed that nearly all terrestrial life goes forward or backward, goes up or down, but rarely, if ever, sideways? It is considered a malfunction almost.'

'What about dancing? Tangos, for instance?'

'Dancing, yes, but that is not considered a usual gait.'

Lena was getting impatient.

'Honor, I'm hungry. If Jeff's rotten parcel does not come today, I will give somebody something!'

I wanted to say 'Tch! Tch!' but I was hungry also. We now had our backs to the window. Preparations had begun for supper, which would be served in almost half an hour.

'You want a brief synopsis, Lena, to reason with, is it?'

'No, just to see if I'm right – I'm not an aboriginal yet.'

'Well, if Adam's spare ribs were, possibly, wings, then God may have clipped them to earth-train Adam and Eve. He created Eve to assist Adam in his new role, as first steward of the land. Adam may originally have had those spare or floating ribs attached, hinge-like, as wings! But because God had created a terrestrial Eve for him, he would learn to live with Eve, in the garden earth. God wanted earth men, so he eliminated from his formula the sky factor, the power Adam once had, perhaps, of physically vacating the earth.'

'God! I am tired,' said Lena, laughing. 'Honor, to say the least of it, it's novel anyway!'

'The possibilities there are limitless,' I said.

I felt relieved now I had talked. It passed the time and kept the mind alert, I thought. I had not spoken for two days until then. That night I slept soundly. I was spiritually and emotionally spun out.

'Honor, are you out of your mind!'

I answered brightly, falsetto voice.

'You know the old saying, Mother – "Show me your company and I'll show you what you are".'

I did not believe that, but Mother chose to ignore it.

'What an idea,' she said. 'How did you expect to get to the bishop's palace, and for what, pray?'

'Not exactly the bishop's palace, Mother.'

I tried to explain. I told her how miserable I had been after she had left, that I felt useless, for I felt it was so unnecessary for me to remain on, and yet I could not go. I explained how I intended to escape, to go away, find work, and never return again. When I came to the scene of the boot of the chaplain's car, Mother turned pale but still said nothing.

'So you see, Mother, it was just a temptation. I did not do it and nobody accused me either.'

She stood up. We were in the waiting room, where I received my visitors now I was up and about. 'Mother, please don't go yet. Why are you in such a hurry today?'

'I'm going to see the doctor, Honor. I can't understand how he could allow you to do such a thing. You might have smothered to death.' She turned and said to me with dramatic dignity: 'Remember, Honor, don't say anything, anything, remember, to anyone about this.'

Mother pulled on her chamois gloves fiercely. I realised I should have kept my big mouth shut. I tried to pass the whole thing off as a joke, but Mother was on the warpath. 'I'm really in a hurry, Honor. I'm getting a lift back and I have to go to the doctor first. I'm not having my child getting into boots, and places like that,' she finished lamely.

I was inwardly fuming. Could she not know that all one thinks about here, in the beginning, is release, release, release, until the last nail is finally hammered in.

'Honor, dear, write, and if there is anything worrying you, tell me in the letters.'

'My letters are censored and, would you believe it, Mother, your letters to me are censored too.'

I had hoped to gain an ally. I failed – Mother was unperturbed.

'I am sure it is routine, Honor, that's all. It is not important. Goodbye, dear, until next week.'

Chapter 10

I went up the green passage, and through the door with the glass top. I was dazed and annoyed because of my stupidity. Lena had just played out one of her scenes. She had commenced as I left for the visitors' room. She had the timid Mrs Crane on a chair, and was telling her, in a Mrs Advice style:

'Men, dear, are all the same. Certainly, go to the dance and enjoy yourself. I am married and I always go to the dances here. The few that there are anyway. Get yourself a man, Mrs Crane, that will make him come running. Isn't that right, Honor?' She laughed over at me.

She came over to me, with a cat-like tread, forgetting about poor Mrs Crane, who had not yet decided for or against Lena's proposition. I was seated in a chair by the window, as usual. She sat beside me.

'Honor, there is a dance tonight, after supper, 7pm to 11pm, for the patients. Are you going?'

I did not reply immediately. Lena laughed self-consciously.

'Well I am going anyhow, Honor. This place gives me the creeps.'

I was suddenly interested. So she had noticed that it was sinister, depressing and foreboding – all those people waiting to be tortured, and nobody with the courage to object. That nurse at the table was writing one of her reports, using words she was trained to use, their code. I knew, I had once read part of a report book secretly, damning words like 'schizophrenia', 'paranoia', 'melancholia'. All stupid, utterly irrelevant to whimsical nature. The funny thing about those words, they just did not seem to fit those quiet, silent patients who were thus categorised. I realised Lena was asking me a question.

'Dance? Is there dancing here?'

'Of course. They have just begun the season, to warm us up.'

She looked at me intently, intuitively.

'Cheer up, Honor, come to the dance. All are invited, admission is free. Get yourself a man for two hours. Anything in trousers will do me, I'm not particular.'

Tibby sidled up. There were curlers in her hair, and a bright green necklace ornamented her thin, angular neck. Two bangles swirled around her thin wrists. Already she was dressed up for the dance. She sported a pink satin dress, almost to her calves, and the belt around her waist was of red, shiny plastic. She wore sandals, and suntan cosmetic on her face and legs. Her arms were very white, and she had either run out of suntan or she intended 'tanning' later.

Lena looked at Tibby.

'Hello, getting ready for bed, Tibby?'

Tibby disregarded the ambiguity.

'You could do with a few curlers yourself, Lena, couldn't she, Honor?'

'Cheeky, it's not the hair men want,' Lena answered quickly.

'Lena, I think I will go. I haven't much style. What are you wearing?' I said.

'Jumper and skirt. I'm a sensible married woman.'

I inspected the few garments I had with me, and decided to wear the blue poplin dress. It had big white flower splashes on it. I put on plenty of lipstick, as I was pale from the day's unexpected annoyances and misunderstandings.

After supper, a small band of us left the admission ward. Ten minutes walking brought us to the patients' dance hall. It had a good floor. Almost a thousand people were there altogether and the band was playing a foxtrot when we arrived. A presiding matron and a psychiatrist sat at the entrance side door, facing down towards the band and the dancers, chatting and observing. Lena and I sat on two vacant chairs. Directly, an odd-looking little man ran across to Lena and asked her, very precisely, to dance.

'Yes, darling,' Lena replied, in her most gasping, insincere manner. As she left, she winked at me and said, 'Mind you get a dancer, Honor, not a prancer!'

It was all very strange to me, but better than the wards, more life, more hope. It was my first time there, so I decided to wait for a Paul Jones. If romance blossoms here, I thought, it is truly on thorns and thistles . . .

It was at the dance that you kept in touch, found an admirer if you could, and so began a futile romance. I was no exception. I found my admirer, or rather, he found me. He walked directly over to me and indicated rather peremptorily that he would like the pleasure of my company. He had an intense, one-woman manner, but his clothes were casual – a loose tweed jacket and grey flannel pants. His shirt was white. I cannot recall his tie or even if he wore one, but if he did, claret or wine was the colour. I remember especially his eyes. He had a way of looking at you, with his ice-blue eyes – they brooked no refusal.

My blue eyes looked up and they said 'Yes'. Talking isn't done. I was in his arms, all my worries forgotten, concentrating only on this man, dancing, and the music. My reddish golden hair was in a roll, almost touching my shoulders. It was a quickstep. From the beginning, he held me closely, but as the dance continued, and we continued without changing partners, he held me so close to him that dancing became of secondary importance, but I knew, and he knew, that we both enjoyed an unconventional intimacy – wordless. He did not know that he supplied just what I needed then, reassurance that I was desirable. He boosted my deflated ego, and uplifted my female morale. The attraction between us was satisfying, for my part, because it was purely physical to me, and apparently to him. I had not to drop handkerchiefs, and he had not to 'box clever'. I wondered why he was unmarried, for he had strong sexual impulses, obviously. After some years, I met and danced sometimes with one of his friends. He had not many. His friend told me he was of a well-to-do, respectable family. I could see no reason for his being there.

He failed to turn up once, at a dance I went to. I missed him, but I had some substitutes. I danced with one, his friend. He said

'Ice-Blue' was not allowed go to the dance because he had smuggled in some drink, and the white coats had to lock him in his room. I feigned indifference. His friend assured me that he, 'Ice-Blue', would think of me continually in his room, especially if he sobered and realised he had missed the dance. I felt sorry, but I did not like the idea of being in his room, in his thoughts, while he could not get out.

Refreshments were served to all at half-time. Lena sat down beside me for tea. She gave a few little gasps of secret triumph. Her eyes were no longer a broody brown, but black and sparkling. She was in a mood.

'Enjoying the dance, Lena?'

'Marvellous, sweetheart. Terrific band, isn't it?'

I nodded approvingly. We were trying to sip tea, genteelly, from large mugs. Lena produced a cigarette and a match out of her clothes. She chuckled and said:

'There's a fella there, Honor, who thinks I'm single. Well, I'm for what they think I am, better sport. He wants to take my temperature. He's either damned clever or an idiot. He's got a thermometer, one he pinched, I suppose, in his pocket, and,' she burst out laughing, . . . 'he says that the rule here is to take the temperature under the arm, or in the groin.' She chuckled again. 'Cheeky, but I'll lead him up the garden path, next dance.'

'How? what do you mean, Lena?'

'Ha! That's my secret,' she said.

The band rose. The small man came over again. As she followed him, Lena cast me back a mischievous glance, and said *sotto voce*: 'Watch my Highland fling!'

I reflected. I was becoming more introspective each day. I watched them. Yes, the little man was curiously like a business-like fox terrier, gambolling now, ludicrously, with the feline Lena to a sudden 'request tango'. Lena had somehow adopted a mask which was 'foxy'. A few more fleeting glimpses I had of the incompatible pair and then they disappeared in the crowd.

Chapter 11

Ice-Blue had disappeared temporarily, I noted, probably to the 'men's'. From time to time, female patients sat beside me and talked and were very sociable. There were so many Paul Jones dances that everybody had the opportunity of dancing. I stopped opposite a female patient in one of the Paul Jones, and as no male rescued either of us, we danced together.

'Are you long here?', I asked.

'Yes, I'm a parole. That tells you, doesn't it?'

'Do you like it here?'

'I have to. My uncle's here. He's paroled too. My name's Delia. What's yours?' She spoke in an attractive staccato way.

Her long oily, flaxen hair gleamed in the electric light and moved gently around her head as she danced. As she danced she talked. Dancing to Delia was a social function, and she talked as effortlessly as she danced, but with a subtle dominance: in giving a cue, intended to extract something else from conversation other than information, something intangible. It might have been a certain timbre of voice, or resonance, she was seeking. Her face was very pale and her eyes were large and blue, but she rarely opened them fully. Her mouth was her most unusual feature. It was as if God in a humorous mood had only carved it in outline. You felt she never experienced pleasure from it, such as eating or drinking, and as for kissing, one could never imagine her putting it to that impractical use.

I danced the next dance with Ice-Blue. I could see Delia above the dancers, just a few feet away. She was dancing what Ice-Blue and I should be dancing – a slow waltz.

48

Delia and her partner glided on, almost cheek to cheek. He was tall and dark and he had horn-rimmed spectacles. They glided sensuously, as if they were in a dream. He was dominant now, or was it she? And then suddenly I saw, I knew, what Delia's mouth reminded me of – a lioness's mouth. Yes, she was rather like a lioness, the very mouth. It was her blond hair which had confused me, for flaxen hair hardly suggests leonine comparisons. It was not her mouth which was the incongruity, it was her camouflage.

The last dance was almost over. Ice-Blue, silent as a lama, was more intense now, and we danced unaware of our feet. At the end, he squeezed my two biceps, which I interpreted as 'It won't be long now, soon.' Then he left me abruptly and disappeared among the men. It was over.

Old shabby coats appeared, as if from nowhere. There was a continuous exodus of males and females from their respective sides of the hall. At the doors, the human sheep were counted and sepa-rated into flocks. The bandsmen were talking together as they put their instruments into cases. Soon, the electric yellow glare would go out and a deserted hall would remain, save for a few cleaners, to sweep, shine, and prepare it for the morning. It would resume its normal, practical function – male and female dining room.

Lena linked arms with Tibby and me. Our group, the admis-sion group, left together, two nurses at the head and two at the rear. It was as bright as day outside, although November, for the moon shone brightly, and the stars sparkled like gems.

'Did you get a fella, Honor?' Tibby began. On Lena's face was a moonlit smirk, and she dealt deftly and quickly, as usual, with what she used to describe as 'Tibby's impertinence'.

'Of course she did. A parole conquest, wasn't it, Honor. I used to know that fella's name. He's been here – years. Didn't he tell you, Honor?'

I remembered him as Ice-Blue but I could not say this to Lena. I said, as if indifferent: 'There was nobody to introduce us.'

Tibby giggled sarcastically.

'Introductions? In here? Did he say, "May I have the honour?"'

This ambiguity proved too much for Lena. She removed her arm from Tibby's and hissed sibilantly at her:

'Oh go to . . . ! You're always trying to be smart. We enjoyed it, even if you didn't.'

We had gone up the green hall, and were passing through the glass-topped door of the admission building. I spoke with relief and with regret.

'Here we are again. If we had our escorts with us now, Tibby, we would have different stories to tell tomorrow, wouldn't we, Lena?'

'Yes,' said Tibby, regretfully.

'What of it, good times will come,' said Lena.

'If I had my parole . . .' Tibby began.

'Yes, 'if," said Lena.

There was a silence, while the door was slammed and locked behind us.

'Yes, if you had your parole,' continued Lena, 'you would meet your boilerman again, or some other poor fish, and lose the parole all over again.' Tibby defended herself.

'There's spies everywhere. But I'm well up now. Catch me!'

We quickly stripped and nightdressed in the locker room. We went back on tiptoe to the inner sanctum, the darkened dormitory, through the observation ward and beyond the ECT ward. We found our beds without putting on the lights, for the moon streamed in through the unfrosted top half of the windows. We could see and sense the sleepless, heartbroken martyrs, listening, unable to shut out the snores or bores from their active minds.

'Pleasant dreams,' said Lena.

'Pleasant dreams,' Tibby and I whispered back.

The next day, to keep from thinking, I helped with numerous chores. I did all the casual jobs which did not commit me to a schedule. I thought of going to the sewing room, for a day or two, just for a change. I thought it might be a stimulating experience. There were probably many eccentrics there, and it might prove helpful, or at least interesting.

But I decided not to go. If I went, I would have to forsake my attitude of temporary preparedness for immediate departure. I would automatically commit myself to a community spirit then prevailing. In such circumstances, I did not wish to spend one minute longer than I could help in the Big House. If I did go, Mother would procrastinate further, and I might almost have to serve a term of apprenticeship there. I could not see any priority release given on those grounds. At the moment it was my prerogative to divert myself. No. I would stay where the official comings and 'goings-on' were. I had my fingers on the pulse. I was geared to demand my release of every visiting doctor or authority, at every single available opportunity. They would realise, the psychiatrists, by my persistence, that I was dead in earnest, and that my reflexes were geared to instant departure. I only wanted my release. I was not prepared to pretend, to compromise, to waste time in their nirvana, doing unpaid, unsuitable work, to attain distinctions of power for services rendered. From my point of view they had 'shanghaied' me. I thought also that the psychiatrist might become human with contact, and have compassion on me, that he might even relax the rules and insist on Mother taking me home there and then. How wrong I was. Patients were grist to their mill. Pick or choose – 'the treadmill' or the 'bird's nest soup'.

The superintendent came unexpectedly to the admission on Saturday afternoon. I wanted satisfaction, so I approached him as politely and deferentially as I could manage. I explained, needlessly, that I had finished the treatment, and that I now expected to leave, at the next board meeting.

'Tch! Tch!' he said. I must have interrupted his contemplations. 'Honor, I have seen your mother . . .' He coughed irritably, as if cornered, and, if I remember Mother, I expect he was. He coughed again, smoothed his old school tie. I noticed how his linen shone and dazzled from the borax gloss I now knew how to apply.

'What's this I hear about us going to escape again?'

'"Us"?' I said.

'You, of course, Honor. You cannot be in a good frame of mind, to contemplate that.'

I knew in a flash. Mother had 'grassed' on me. I felt my cheeks burning, and I exploded in wrath.

'Frame? Frame? This whole place is a frame. A frame-up. Everybody is framed.'

He appeared amused but I did not care.

'Come now, Honor. I think we will send you to the USA. You will have to steady up. We cannot have you breaking out or running away. Your mother says you might do something desperate, so, to avoid unpleasantness, since we are far too busy with the treatments to chase after patients here, I have arranged for you, with your mother's consent of course, to go over to the Long Trench division on Sunday.'

I burst out crying.

'Tch! Tch! Honor, we can't have you crying.'

A nurse who was hovering nearby approached him and I heard him say the words grams or grains. I checked my sobs and sat down, staring, unbelieving, after his disappearing figure. The nurse came over to me and asked me to take a tablet. It must have been a sedative. She handed me a glass of water. I swallowed it, not caring. I looked desperately around the admission. Nobody seemed to care or know how I was feeling, or that I had received another mortal blow, and I was reeling. They were sending me to Long Trench block tomorrow, Sunday, in the evening, probably after Mother's visit. She had inadvertently done this to me.

Chapter 12

The next day, Sunday morning, I was told by the matron to gather my belongings together, as I was going to Long Trench block at 3pm. She also added, to my dismay, that my mother had phoned to say that she could not come to see me that Sunday, and not to be disappointed, that she would come in the following Sunday. I nodded dumbly. I understood. There was no escape. I had to go. The matron, having done her good deed, departed on her rounds.

I sat at the table beside the glass-topped door for lunch. Noise and shouts could be heard from the ward below. It sounded like a revolt, and I hoped Lena was not involved. In spite of revolts we had to eat, so we began lunch, hungrily. Suddenly, one of the new patients rushed into the room. Two nurses, minus their caps, were in hot pursuit. She wore a dressing gown, but she was bare-footed. She saw the door and ran towards me. Perhaps she thought I was in her way to freedom, as I was almost beside the door, for she grabbed me from behind, and a tug-of-war developed between her and my hair. I tried to ease matters by various means, but she knocked me over backwards, or, rather, pulled me back by my long hair as I tried to free myself. A leg broke off the chair, and I fell back on the splintered joint of the leg. As I fell, the two nurses loosened her hands from my hair and I was freed.

I was shaken, but I could feel no anger against her, for I guessed she had probably reached the end of her tether. I remembered how I felt, on my admission. She seemed to realise it was no use, for she allowed a nurse to lead her back to bed. The other nurse examined me with temporary haste, and pronounced me unharmed. I could not, in decency, show her the place where it hurt, which was very tender indeed. Later on, a purple photograph of a splinter appeared on my posterior.

On account of that incident, I no longer felt like visiting the dormitory to say goodbye to all the patients I knew there. I had intended doing this, but now I felt sore, disturbed and very near to tears, so I sat miserably by the window awaiting my transfer. I expected a nurse now any minute, to take me, my charts and my case history to Long Trench. At 3pm exactly we left, she carrying the incriminating documents, and I my case of belongings. On the avenue outside, I looked back, and I could see Lena and Tibby at a window. As I waved, many more patients crowded to the windows, no doubt wondering where I was going. I knew Lena would tell them, afterwards, her own version of my transfer. I felt sad. I had some friends there, and who knew what lay ahead of me in Long Trench, for rumour had it at that time that few go in, but none go out.

There were two entrances to Long Trench. The nurse took me in the back entrance. I was officially handed over, there, to the charge nurse. She was in her office, which was simply a converted small cell. There was a white medicine chest, a writing desk which was really a table, and all sorts of odds and ends.

The charge nurse, who was sitting inside, was sour and surly looking. I thought her heavy-lidded eyes were cunning and sadistic, but she veiled them quickly, so that it was difficult to ascertain her expression. Her face was as white as skimmed milk. She deliberately ignored me, and I stood there with the admission nurse, wondering what I should do. She had written into a book the inventory of my things.

She closed the book, took out a cigarette and lit it. Most nurses are friendly to each other, but she addressed the nurse officiously, and the young nurse seemed relieved to go. She scurried out and I was left alone with the 'Big Boss'. She surveyed me contemptuously from under her heavy lids. Her whole attitude was contempt. She smoked for a few seconds, blew a cloud of smoke in my face and spoke:

'"Honor". Is that all?'

'Honor Tassel,' I said.

In that instant of introduction, I knew that, here, in Long Trench, I had been selected indiscriminately, to be provoked and humiliated by this six-foot ring-mistress. She was horsey; even the very shape of her face was equine. Her voice was chilling, sepulchral, as whitewashed as all the tiny white cells around. It was as if she put a cold hand around my heart when she spoke to me – as if I were a cadaver and she an anatomist. I dropped my suitcase and began to shift from one foot to the other, waiting for her orders. She spoke abruptly, almost disdainfully.

'Do you masturbate?'

'What!' I said, astonished.

'. . . because, if you do, you will have to sleep in an open dormitory. On the other hand, I have only one spare cell left, and if you don't, you may have it, provided you give no trouble.'

She paused to remove her cigarette, which had stuck to her equine mouth.

'Oh! I wouldn't do that,' I said timidly.

'Well, that's settled then,' she said. She stubbed her cigarette regretfully.

'You won't need your case. You can leave it here. I have to check it with the inventory. I will label it so it can't be lost, and if there is anything you want out of it, I will give it to you. Understand?'

'Yes, thank you,' I answered.

'Come on then, I'll show you to your cell, and you can make your bed up before you go to supper.' I followed, in her six-foot shadow, along the passage, aptly called the Long Trench, of thirty or forty whitewashed dugouts, glaring white. There were four large dormitories interspersed between them. All the sleeping cells and rooms were on one side, and nothing but chairs and barred windows with tiny panes of glass on the opposite side. The only ventilation, apart from the passage draughts, was from slits of an inch, high up in the windows. The air slots were permanently open because they could not be closed. It was all right for winter, but inadequate for summer. The 'Big Boss' stopped at a cell. I looked in fearfully. Inside was an iron bed, and on it a striped horse-hair mattress, pillows, a bolster and some thin, folded blankets. The iron-framed window was, as all the others, a secure, immovable fixture, designed to imprison.

She pointed at the wire cage shutters.

'All shutters are locked every night, and the door,' she said.

There was a peep-hole in the wooden door, and a wire-slatted grill beneath, for extra air I presumed. I asked, unnecessarily:

'What is the round hole in the door for?'

'To see you are there,' she said grimly. 'The night nurse looks in every two hours.'

She departed then, to my relief. I felt uneasy, and her domineering attitude made me nervous. A minute later, a small, timid, lame patient left two sheets and pillow cases on my bed. She said not a word. I discovered later that she was dumb. I made up my bed and looked distastefully at the extra chattels left there for the night. I thought the huge flannelette nightdress looked ridiculous, and I wanted my pyjamas and dressing gown and slippers. I will ask for them later on, I decided.

I wandered outside, to see if I could find any nice people about. There were dozens of people outside in the Trench. Some were sitting in groups of three or four, some were sitting alone, others were walking. Some walked up and down purposefully, but I discovered later it was to keep warm. Nearly everybody looked strange, in their clothes, their manner, their speech. They were very different from the admission patients. It was a few days before I made any friends at all. My first approaches that day were rejected with suspicion. Some spoke angrily to me, others stared blankly or aghast at me, as if I were a ghost or a freak.

'No Hope Hold', the chief security ward, was directly beneath Long Trench. The female padded cells were there, and other similar detention cells. I had heard it all from time to time from old lags. The strait-jacket was used in the Hold and sedatives and other special drugs. Long Trench block was joined to No Hope Hold by a slanted passage. It was like the hold of a ship, with caged windows. Strict security precautions and punishment were the order of the day. If you were in Long Trench, it was said, and you as much as raised your voice, you might be seized immediately by four or five nurses and rushed below to No Hope Hold. There, you were tamed or shamed, to become dispirited and hopeless. You would meet there the cream of the Big House, the wild indomitables, the super eccentrics, the dreamers who no longer wanted reality. Strange, though, the pot did not call the kettle black there. It just nodded and said, 'Hello – you're sooty too.'

Chapter 13

One person who did speak to me that day was Oonagh. She was to be found nearly always beside the fireplace. A large fireguard was padlocked to each wall, on each side of the fireplace. Oonagh usually stood by this fireguard, as its keeper, or else as a self-appointed sentinel.

There was a chair nearby, and I sat there and looked up at Oonagh. She clutched the fireguard like an eagle, her fingers interlaced with the bracketing. For minutes she stared down into the gloomy fireplace, and then she swung around swiftly, like a professional dancer, and scrutinised all who were near her sacred eyrie. She had almost a sneer on her face, yet there was a certain bleakness in her expression that belied the sneer. I discovered later that she despised the pretended activity of the patients about her. She disdained any manual labour herself, and she never exerted herself beyond maintaining her position at the posts she chose to occupy. She was content to portray futility, but she always looked intelligently preoccupied, as if she were about to solve some important problem or mystery of stupendous importance. She had an unusual face, aquiline, almost majestic. At odd moments her black eyes were diamond hard. Her black eyebrows were perfectly shaped. Her hair, before she cut it herself finally, was plaited in a loosely made coil on her neck. She persisted in a steadfast independence of attitude, an aloofness, at the expense of a certain unapproachable loneliness. Sometimes she sought diversion, as if she dared not go any further in her speculations. The black eyes would glint, she would unbend, actually stoop, to address, to please. A steady smile would appear on her lips, lighting her whole, dark, strange personality. The smiling face is a mask she adopts to feign interest. The interest may be motivated by pity or condescension, but she studies the art before the action. She has not found the answer.

I sat on a creaky, varnished chair, within speaking distance.

'The fire, do you have one here, then?'

'Oh yes,' she replied. 'Not for another week though.'

A little further down, high up on the wall out of arm's reach, was a large roman-lettered clock. It read five. The door under it opened, and a group of twenty or thirty patients entered. They seemed timid and subdued, except for two girls. One was laughing and the other replied, animatedly, concerning a film they had seen. I remembered then that the 'pictures' had commenced this Sunday.

'Don't you go to the pictures?' I asked.

'No,' came the reply. 'They're not real, are they? What good are they?'

'Well, I suppose they help you to forget, for a time.'

'Oh? Yes? But they don't, do they?'

Just then two patients approached, laughing, talking, reminiscing. One was plump and made up, the other was soap-washed, small and gentle. They were the youngest I had seen in Long Trench yet, about the same age as myself. The plump girl spoke first.

'I'm Bessie. I saw you in church. Welcome over.'

'I'm Kathleen,' said the other. 'Are they crowded out in admission again?'

'Yes,' I smiled. 'It's the phase of the new moon. I'm Honor. What's it like over here?'

Bessie lowered her voice cautiously before she replied.

'Mind your Ps and Qs here.'

'That's a nice name, Honor,' Kathleen said gently. She looked up at the clock. 'Supper's at six.'

I felt very weary and tired, more in mind than in body, and I decided I would go to bed immediately after supper, hoping it would refresh me and prepare me for adapting to my new quarters.

As I walked in the direction of my room, a very old lady hailed me and introduced herself. She was the oldest patient there, I found out later. She sat on a divan, which was a converted bedspring on legs, on top of which was a mattress covered by a faded floral coverlet. She was unravelling wool, scrap, from a grey cotton bag, and winding it into small multi-coloured balls. She had wispy, thin grey hair. Her twinkling blue eyes searched my face wisely and kindly.

'Hello, darlin', I'm Rosie,' she said.

'Hello, Rosie, I'm Honor.'

'What brought a nice girl like yourself over here to this place?'

'It's a long story, I might tell you some time,' I said, looking down at her upturned, quizzical face. She caught the bag of wool nearer to her, patted the divan on which she sat alone.

'Sit down here, darlin'. You know you can stay up for another hour if you wish.'

'Oh I don't know. I haven't been told the rules here yet. You are a parole I suppose?'

'Just a semi, it's not official, you understand.'

'Why "semi"? Surely at your age . . .'

'Well, you see, darlin' . . .' she broke a bit of wool . . . 'Drat it. It's like this, a little incident about forty years ago, no, let me see, maybe fifty. It's in the books you see.'

'But at your age, surely you could go home.'

'Ah, indeed! God help your sense, child, I have no home to go to now.'

'Oh!' I said, 'what age are you then?'

'Eighty-two and a bit. Most of my age group are in Sunset House.'

'Is that a nice place?'

'Child,' she leaned closer and whispered, 'They want me to retire and go over. Just an old wooden shack. I would not go.' She wound the wool with slow, deliberate movements. 'I have some say. They take my pension, you know, for my keep.'

'All of it?'

'Yes, but I manage to earn a few bob in the laundry. Listen, darlin', you ought to come to the laundry, it will get you away from her.'

She indicated the Big Boss's office, and returned to her wool-winding, after turning down her lips and grimacing suitably.

'Don't worry, she won't bully me,' I said.

'You don't know her like I do. Be careful, child. What sort of work did you do before you came in here?'

'Nothing much. When I left school I did a little nursing. During the war.'

'Ah! I once had a boy, a sweetheart, you know. He was a soldier, and he went to the wars and I never saw him again. Of course, that's a very long time ago. Never mind, darlin'. You will have your purgatory over you,' she said, consolingly.

'I'm not supposed to go to purgatory,' I said.

Her eyes rounded in surprise, and I explained wryly.

'Rosie, don't you know that if you go to confession, and holy communion, and pray for the holy father's intentions, you gain a plenary indulgence. That means you go straight there, to heaven.'

'Ahem,' Rosie gave a little discreet cough. 'I did forget, Honor, but I seldom go to church nowadays, but you could offer your plenary indulgence for some poor sinner.'

'Rosie, what brought you here?'

'Ah, child, that's a long story.'

She wound her last ball of wool and began to hum, and partly sing, an old sad song about 'a soldier boy'. I got up.

'It's time I went to bed. Goodnight, Rosie.'

'Mind what I said, careful. Goodnight darlin'.'

I did not sleep at all. The rooms looked deceptively soundproof, as if they were solid cave structures, but that was only an illusion due to the cold, icy-looking whitewash. Actually the walls were so thin that the only privacy they gave was to the sight. The patient sleeping next to me spent every minute of the entire night singing mad old shanties, or screeching wild hysterical laughter. In between songs, if songs they could be called, she emitted challenging, ghoulish calls that were spine-chilling. On the other side of me resided *per nocte* another contradictory individual. She talked non-stop the entire night, absurdities, fantastic stringing of words, as if she were reading the Bible, or the Koran, in an unalterable monotone. I knocked on both walls, and from one came an unmistakable whoop of joy. She knocked in return, with interest, curiosity and disappointment, for ten minutes. The knock on the other side produced the effect I feared: a dead stop for three minutes, then a resumption of the epic or whatever it was.

My eyes were dark with insomnia the next morning. I noticed that the monotonous one spoke not at all, she was as silent as the proverbial tomb. Her hair was tied back with a bow behind, like a judge, and she looked severe and disciplined. The other bouncing night-lover did not speak either. Both kept to themselves. Thinking of the night shift no doubt.

Chapter 14

Rosie advised me, after breakfast, to ask to go with the nurse for the messages. She said that this walk would be 'one of the privileges'.

'Right,' I said and suited the action to the word. I asked the Boss in such a way as to suggest prompting.

'May I go with the nurse for the messages?'

She dilated her nostrils and considered.

'Yes, I suppose you can. Be ready, and don't delay her.' Rosie murmured satisfaction when I told her.

'So far, so good,' she said cynically. 'Watch her, mind.' She took out a box, and took a large pinch of snuff, and sniffed it expertly into each nostril. 'Honor, before you go, you're not one of the suicidal patients, are you?' She looked anxiously at me. 'There's many here,' she said sadly.

'No, of course not,' I said.

Poor, dear Rosie, I wonder how she is. I hope they did not send her to Sunset House. Many of the pals she had are there. She remained, to work all her life in the laundry. The first thing I did when I left the rehabilitation centre was to buy a bottle of tonic wine and send it to Rosie. I chuckled as I packed and addressed it. I knew she would imagine herself the pope then. When I attained parole, two years before I left the Big House, I occasionally took back a glass of brandy to Rosie from the town. It was a sacrifice, as I seldom earned, unofficially, more than ten shillings a week, ironing dance frocks for the nurses. Such little, illicit pleasures cemented our friendship down the years. I took a risk, because, if it was reported, I would be penalised. But Rosie was the soul of discretion, full of wiles, humour and dry wit. She was diplomatic, but you never guessed it. She was on everybody's side, as one often is who has nothing to lose and nothing to gain.

My first privilege, when I went with a nurse for the messages, proved disappointing, except for one minor incident. I met Ice-Blue, my faithful dancing partner, in the hospital sweetshop. He was buying cigarettes. He remembered me, in his own peculiar fashion. Nothing was said, but his eyes spoke, and I understood he looked forward to the next dance. Woman's intuition. We left quickly, the nurse and me, as is customary on the messages. I carried the basket, full of confectionery and similar goods, while she carried charts, notes, diet boards and shoes. We went next to the bread store, where I saw the huge bread slicers in action. The workers were very quiet, paroled patients. Then we went to the shoe repair shop, the carpentry shop, general stores, fetching charts and goods, and leaving notes and charts.

When we arrived at the big kitchen, steam was rising from monster-sized cauldrons of soup. I noticed paroled patients were helping everywhere, but they had a dependent, dejected look on their faces, almost as if they regretted compromising the part for the whole. They were silent and introspective, as they washed up, or washed vegetables, or did any of the various menial chores involved in the maintenance of three thousand patients.

When the nurse and I arrived back with the messages, I learned from a patient that the letter post had been given out. The Boss summoned me to her now laconic presence. She spoke as if she had a hot potato, not a bit, in her mouth.

'Honor, there's a letter for you.'

She handed me the censored slit envelope. I wondered had she read it. I took it delightedly with me to a corner. Mother was not feeling well. She had been advised by our doctor at home not to travel for another week. She said she would send me the parcel, and that I was not to be too disappointed.

I was disappointed. I shed a few silent tears in the corner and put the letter away in my bag.

For meals, I trooped down with the others to the mixed dining hall. The men were a sea of faces in the daylight on the other side of the hall. On my side, I was among hundreds of women I had never seen until then, neither at church, on the walks or at the dance. They shunned society and diversion, but food was a priority. They had to eat, and were unable to protest or refuse or sustain rebellion for long. They were broken in, but it only needed a tiny spark for the conflagration. A patient would snatch her neighbour's food, to offend or provoke. Many patients took handfuls of waste out of the waste buckets, and had to be 'cleaned' afterwards. Many confusing incidents like this happen, but they are ignored and go uninvestigated.

I recall one patient who confused me by her behaviour. One day, I was alone with her in a small day-room. She attacked me, beat me, and pulled my hair. I could do nothing, as she was an epileptic patient, and I feared if I defended myself properly, as I was perfectly capable of doing, she might have a fit, which could be fatal. She stopped after a few minutes, and I offered her my hand and said I was sorry. She accepted my apology with extreme bashfulness and apologised also.

At that time, there was no recreation, as recreation now is understood. There were only long, dreary crocodile walks. The dances, as recreation, were useless, as they were too infrequent to be of real therapeutic value. They provided for most just a small taste of the delectables they imagined.

After lunch, a list of names was taken of patients who wished to go to the pictures that afternoon. The films were always shown in the dance hall, or my dining hall as it was now. I gave my name, although I was tired and weary from lack of sleep, and this I considered not my fault, but the faults of my two exuberant neighbours. I remember how Rosie described her own tiredness to me once rather picturesquely.

'Darlin', I'm so tired I could sleep on a harrow.'

In spite of my fatigue, and my sad disappointment from the letter, I went to the pictures with the other pleasure seekers. I found a vacant chair at the back, at the end of a row. The first row of the men was behind. A long table served as barricade between the species. One or two vacant chairs were to my left. A man arrived late, and he put one of those chairs beside mine and occupied it. I ignored him, as he seemed fully absorbed in the Western film before us. After about ten minutes, just as I had forgotten him, I felt his hand sliding into the side pocket of my coat. Nobody noticed, as he appeared to be still absorbed in the picture. After a short time he withdrew his hand before I could say or do anything. A few minutes later, and his hand was again in my pocket, a cautious pressure was applied and then it withdrew. I felt I should do something, but what? Should I stand up, and report him to the white coats gleaming three rows back, or should I assume and hope that the fascination my pocket had for him had evaporated, was no more? If I reported him, he would be penalised far in excess of his idiotic behaviour.

As I deliberated on my next course of action, I involuntarily put my hand into my pocket and met his going out. I looked obliquely at this sex-starved Fabian, and I felt – remorse. My fingers touched something metallic at the base of my pocket. My pocket had been empty. It felt like two small coins, one bigger than the other. I took them out, and examined them curiously in the light available from the screen. A shilling and a sixpenny bit. I put my hand back in my pocket, the coins clenched in my fist. I should have felt angry with him, or insulted, but I did nothing. Then, as his hand slid over mine, I put the coins in his hand. He took them and withdrew his hand. I sensed his disappointment, his failure. I was relieved. At last I had done something, and with, I thought, a certain amount of dignity. The lights went on. The surreptitious romancer had vacated his seat, wisely, a few seconds before.

I secretly congratulated myself for having dealt with a unique problem in a unique manner. There was no extra scene, either, and the incident was closed as far as I was concerned. I returned to Long Trench, to our own particular make-believe world.

That same Sunday evening, I knocked at the door of the Big Boss's office.

'Please, Nurse, may I have my dressing gown, pyjamas and slippers from my case.'

She smoked her cigarette viciously, and gulped a mouthful of white tea.

'I can't see why you can't be the same as everyone else here, and wear house clothes. I will send them down to your cell later on. Well, what are you waiting for,' she shouted, 'be off!'

'It is impossible to sleep in that cell. Nurse, the noise . . .' I explained.

'You're not in the admission now. I can't give you a sedative here at night, or order it. If you can't sleep and want sedatives, you will have to go to the Hold.'

'The noise is continuous, Nurse, and I don't really need sedatives. Perhaps if you put me in a quieter cell . . .?'

'No can do,' she grated, decisively, 'no vacancies at the moment. I will mention it to the doctor in the morning. She will only change you below, and you will sleep less there, it's noisy, and there is the padded cell.'

'Please Nurse, it's all right. Don't mention it to the doctor. They might quieten down.'

I had little hopes of that, but she was not to be diverted.

'Have to! Rules! As you have complained I have to . . . Now go, I am very busy.'

I left her fumbling for her matches. I was furious with myself again. Every impulsive act or thought seemed to produce adverse effects. When I got to my room, I found my dressing gown and my slippers on my bed, but not my pyjamas.

Chapter 15

Monday morning, I made my bed and was tidying and cleaning my room when I was called by a senior nurse and told that the pyschiatrist wanted to speak to me.

I went from my room, and encountered the psychiatrist outside, accompanied by the Boss. I opened my mouth to speak, but before I could say one word, she began hurriedly:

'What's this I hear, Honor, about you not sleeping?' She turned and addressed a suddenly obsequious ring-mistress.

'We can't have that, can we, Nurse?'

There followed a private consultation, as if I were deaf or a sleep-walker. They arrived at some solution by mutual nods, then the psychiatrist resumed her walk as if she had forgotten what I stood for. I intercepted her.

'Doctor, I could go back to the admission or . . .'

'It is all right, Honor. I have arranged for your charge nurse to send you below to the dormitory for a few days' rest.'

I was shocked at this arrangement, and I attempted to voice my protest, but she departed hurriedly, talking to and questioning all the while her escort, the Big Boss, who had her protective instinct in evidence now.

Rosie, Bessie and Kathleen were in the laundry – the talkative ones. I looked down to the fireguard, and Oonagh was there. A small fire burned in the grate, the first since March. It was bad and smoking. Oonagh showed no recognition or interest at my approach. I sat on a chair near her, and waited. I too stared into space, into vacancy.

Suddenly she spoke.

'Are they going to inoculate you, dear?'

She must have seen the doctor talking to me, I guessed.

'No, I don't think so. I had all those things when I was quite young.'

'Everybody gets the needle here. There was a typhoid epidemic here about twenty years ago, and since then everybody is inoculated.'

Big Boss was coming, admonishing, scathing, scolding, in complete control again until the next rounds – Matron's.

She stopped where I sat.

'Doctor's orders. You are to go below for a few days' rest. Mind you behave yourself. If there are any complaints and you give trouble, or show you are not to be trusted, you can't come back here. Understand?'

'Elsewhere, then?' I asked.

'I doubt it.'

So that is why the patients call it No Hope Hold I thought. It is a cul-de-sac, no choice. I felt I wanted air, and I asked timidly: 'May I go on the messages first?'

'No,' her voice was final. 'Undress in your room, and I will take you below personally. You may put on your dressing gown and slippers. Ready, then, after my elevenses.'

She went into her office and closed the door, as if she had completed an exhausting brain operation.

No use at all in arguing, I thought. I undressed and put on my own green dressing gown over the house nightdress. It had lovely quilted satin revers, but it did not look as elegant as it should, and I looked sadly at the monstrous flannelette nightdress which bulged through. My red slippers had serviceable leather heels, and I was glad of their support as I clumsily walked down the Long Trench to 'her' office. The Big Boss was ready. She took my bundle of clothes from me without a word, and threw them into my newly labelled case. She closed the case with frightening finality.

'You will not see many dressing gowns down there,' she said. 'Bath robes.'

'It is only a temporary arrangement,' I said, with what I hoped was dignity in my voice. 'My mother will be here next week, and I expect she will claim me out then. I need a rest, anyhow, before I go home.'

Her voice rose querulously. 'Come on, it's just around the corner.'

So it was. I followed her awkwardly down a slanted tarpaulined passage. She banged impatiently on the inhospitable-looking door at the end, and a frightened nurse opened it about half-way. She was instructed briefly.

'Here, a new one. Doctor says she is to have a few days' rest.'

The sarcastic inflection of the word 'rest' could not be ignored, and the nurse qualified her macabre humour with a nervous, humourless laugh.

'She doesn't know when she's lucky.'

As I went inside, another patient came out, thankful for an unexpected release. I was to occupy her bed, which I saw being prepared for me, with fresh sheets and pillow-cases. It was near the fire, which had the usual locked guard on it. A cloth-covered table and two chairs were placed in front of the fireplace. It was the nurse's official desk, and a ledger-like report book was lying on the table.

Beds were everywhere. There were about ten along both sides of the Hold and a circle of about twenty in the centre. I was on the fire side, facing the six large caged windows. The window mesh was a fixture and allowed in only dim, fractional light. There was plenty of ventilation, as little glass remained, or else never was, in the ceiling-high windows. The bare wooden floorboards were damp now, from recent scrubbing, and smelt strongly of Jeyes fluid. Another odour was obvious, and I recognised it as the paraffin smell from the patients' hair. It was used throughout the Big House as a dandruff remover.

The padded room was locked, but conspicuously silent. Strange sounds were coming from the other detention room. It was locked, unpadded and whitewashed. These white cells were igloo-like, everywhere in the building. The sounds were made by a 'free thinker' inside the igloo. I discovered later that the present occupant, when not muffled in extraneous garments, jumbled somewhere, had certain other extreme ideas, which, fundamentally, would appeal only to a nudist. A fellow-patient had objected to her bohemian demonstration, and had walloped her. She was hurt, so she went into the igloo and 'they' locked the door. She was in for her own safety, the nurse explained to me.

'How do you know when she is all right?' I asked, puzzled.

'Oh she asks for her clothes, and puts on as many layers as an onion.'

Whoever was in the padded cell was still a mystery. A tin plate of food and a spoon were handed in to her at meal times. The last time the nurse opened the door, it was just a few cautious inches, and she employed her feet in the manoeuvre. The plate came flying back over her head, to land in the centre of the Hold, between two beds.

I had an unexpected visitor in the afternoon. Rosie had, by an unofficial and unique privilege, been allowed in to see me. She walked slowly, for she was 'getting on', as she used to say herself. She sat on my bed, thankful for the rest, and did not speak until she had regained her breath.

'Ah, darlin', I just heard. Why on earth did you come down to the 'Hold'?'

I answered quickly, in justification.

'I never intended. I complained of noise beside me at night, and no sleep.'

She looked cautiously around, and when she was satisfied that the nurses were not listening, she whispered, 'There you are, child. I told you. There is not much peace or quiet down here either.' She lowered her voice further. 'Don't let the nurses hear you complaining. They sometimes provoke young lassies like you, just to test you.'

She smoothed her old multi-washed serge and wool housedress with her thin, gentle hands, and deliberately raised her voice for the benefit of the approaching nurse.

'Ah well, darlin', just a few days' rest. I have to go now, to the laundry. By the way, Delia was asking for you.'

'Delia! Who is Delia?'

'She met you at the dance. She says you are a very good dancer, and that it is a pity to see you here.'

I remembered Delia, the girl like a lioness.

'How is she?' I enquired.

Rosie touched her head significantly with her fingers. 'She's not too well up there,' she whispered. 'They want her to take treatment. She has to be locked up sometimes, when she gets "high". Argumentative, you might say.'

'Like what, Rosie,' I said, seeking to detain her, as I wanted to talk.

Rosie's sixth sense warned her that the visiting time allowed her by dint of her semi-parole was over.

'I will say goodbye for the present, darlin'.'

'Goodbye, Rosie. Do they send the post down here?' I called after her.

'Yes, darlin', after lunch they do.'

There was no post for me that day, and the day passed uneventfully enough, except for the strange behaviour and fun-making antics of some of the internees. Some jumped from their beds and ran to the windows, which they shook and rattled, as if to relieve some moments of silence which oppressed them. Others, their food eaten, banged the empty tin plates against the windows. Others, more with irritation than caution, attempted to force the frames with their spoons, and were severely reprimanded, and sometimes slapped, before the two flustered nurses had to devote their energies to some more urgent escapade. A favourite prank of a naughty patient was to smuggle her sheet out to the lavatory and stuff it down the bowl.

There was little cuisine. I had to eat my food off a tin plate with a spoon. Knives and forks were banned there. I drank the usual boiled tea out of an enormous mug. Horrible 'black jack', or cascara (a type of purgative or laxative), was doled out regularly. It was the real, legendary black jack known to some as 'jollop'. It was fascinating to see how some relished it, actually licking their lips as if they would like more. Before I discovered what it was, I was offered a spoonful. Many seemed to enjoy it, so I thought perhaps it was a kind of liquorice. As soon as I tasted it I became violently sick. I was told I turned green. I refused the next offer, and was offered instead a diluted type of cascara from a much bigger bottle. This was generally popular and was given on request.

Chapter 16

Above, in the opposite wards, the patients dressed, worked or walked for exercise through the grounds, supervised. Down here in the Hold were many patients who were half-crippled from their beds, which, as time and the years went on, they refused to leave. Others could not be kept in their beds, grown women, tut-tut, running around playing crazy games of hide and seek, in the lavatories and behind the few and far between corners. The lavatories were around a corner in the dormitory. I cannot say toilets, for there were no wash-basins in those days, before Moses came and struck the rock, and sometimes flooded the place: a new problem.

After supper I saw the occupant of the padded room for the first time. Two nurses led her out, one on each arm. She was small, sturdy and well built, certainly not the emaciated madwoman I half expected to see. She had light brown eyes, of an oblique cast that suggested an Egyptian or an Indian, and she had that peculiar inscrutable expression in her eyes that is attributed to orientals. She seldom spoke, except on one or two occasions, when her placid imperturbability would suddenly change to passionate invective, altering her personality grotesquely. She was young, except for the bitter drooping of the corners of her lips, which gave the impression she was much older, maturer and resigned, which she was not. I learned from Rosie later that she never had visitors. Her relatives had abandoned her.

She came out of the padded room, much like an Indian squaw on the trail, perceiving her surroundings with some sixth sense she had discovered in her gloomy solitude, and clutching modestly around her naked body a thin, yellow faded blanket. Rosie declared that she tore up the clothes they put on her.

Now she stood there, hesitant, seemingly dazzled by the light. She looked intelligently around, her eyes gradually getting into focus. The eyes lingered on me, the newcomer, for a few seconds, then with a sardonic, slightly amused twitching of her lips, she jumped into her bed. She did not lie down, but remained in a sitting posture, as if wondering what had happened in her absence.

I began to tire of looking at others. I drifted into thought, staring into space, not seeing the moving automatons that incessantly moved, but did not move me. Without warning, there was a disturbance, as Sonia, the ex-padded cell patient, jumped from her bed and began to beat up a patient. I looked over at them. It was the patient under the window on the far side. She had been lecturing all day, at half-hourly intervals, talking absolute nonsense. She commanded a minority audience of about ten a day, who suffered her unwillingly. Sonia was not a patient listener. She ran to her, boxed her ears soundly, and began to thump her. The two nurses rushed to her aid, and forced Sonia back into the padded cell. She went with a characteristic bitter twist of her lips, an elusive air of enigmatic triumph in her flashing eyes.

When the night nurses arrived about 8pm, it was fairly quiet. There were occasional shouts of laughter from the locked, unpadded cell, the igloo. I adopted the line of least resistance and took a sedative, for I still hoped to leave and I wanted some sleep first.

I slept heavily and did not wake until the morning. The nurses were making the beds when I awoke. I lay quietly for a few minutes, trying to recollect just what had happened and where I was. Then Sonia bounded out of the padded room and stood enigmatically looking down at me in the bed. I treated her casually, on principle, and rolled over on my right side, turning my back on her unnecessary presence. My laziness, feigned and real, quickly left when Sonia gave two quick whacks to the top of my head with my hard-heeled leather slipper. I sat up quickly. She still had my slipper in her hand, and now she ran around, in and out among the beds. I was furious.

The nurses emerged from the cell, carrying torn strips of blankets. They caught Sonia in full flight, gave me back my slipper and pushed her back into the padded cell. I noticed they put in a different kind of blanket this time, of almost indestructible material, a cold, canvas-like, criss-cross stitched quilt. I heard the nurse say she would have to be given paraldehyde, as she had to be put in too often, and the padded cell had to be kept vacant, if at all possible, for the next emergency. The doctor of course orders the paraldehyde, but it is the nurses who administer it. I had heard of its use here, but I had no actual contact with it until then. After lunch, it was sent down to the Hold on a tray. Two extra nurses were present to assist operations. Sonia was taken from the padded room; I suppose she had no idea of their intentions. She gave vicious little jabs with her elbows as they forced her to her bed. Three nurses held her down, two at the top and one at her feet. The fourth nurse poured the paraldehyde from its bottle into a tall triangular glass, rather like a lager glass.

When Sonia realised their intentions, she struggled and shot glances of hatred at the glass of paraldehyde. They forced her mouth open with an instrument called a gag, or it may have been a tongue depressor, and then they poured the fiery, colourless liquid down her throat. Her struggles increased and increased, almost to frenzy. She was not subject to 'fits' or epilepsy – this was the effect of the paraldehyde. After about twenty minutes, she suddenly went limp and seemed to lose consciousness, while the paraldehyde did its specific work. The fuss was now over. The two extra nurses left the Hold and the others washed their hands in the kitchen, but one came quickly out, while the other prepared a tray for their cuppa.

Everything was in shipshape order when Rosie came to see me again. She had a letter for me.

'Post for you, darlin',' she said. She sat on my bed while I eagerly opened the letter. My tears gathered and dropped onto the page as I read. I read to the end, and then I cried miserably for a full five minutes.

'Poor Honor, is it bad news? What is it, child?'

'Rosie, Mother must be very ill. She has to go to hospital, and she says, she says she may have to have another operation. Rosie, what shall I do if she dies under the operation?'

'Hush, Honor, you are not to think about that. Have faith. It's just that she is lonely without you, and she wants you to think about her and pray for her.'

I stopped crying, and I felt quieter, calmer somehow.

Rosie's calm common sense comforted me, but the letter had shocked me. The fact was that if Mother died, I had nobody to take me out. My brother Paul was now working in an airfield, and he stayed in digs. He had not been to see me, but Mother had explained that.

At 4pm the psychiatrist arrived. She had been told, through Matron's report, that I was 'upset'. Rosie left when the psychiatrist came over to me.

'Now Honor, I heard about your mother. Don't worry, people go to hospital every day. It's the way of the world,' she said. She turned to speak to the nurse standing attentively near us.

'Nurse, give Honor a sedative, it will calm her nerves.'

'Please Doctor, I must write a letter first. Will you post it?' I asked anxiously.

'Of course, Honor, you write lovely letters. Your mother will have it tomorrow.'

I asked the nurse for some paper and pen and ink. I wrote a long letter to Mother, and I resolutely did not refer to my own personal anxieties or troubles. I told her I would pray for her, and that there was nothing I wanted more than to see her well again. I finished the letter without once mentioning where I had been sent – the Hold – but I expect she knew. It would just be another part of the Big House to her, a safe place to keep her darling precious little Honor out of mischief. Then I put it in the envelope and sent it unsealed to the censor's office, for stamping and posting. The nurse gave me a sedative then, and a drink, and very soon I fell fast asleep, from sheer emotional exhaustion and fatigue.

Sonia escaped from the padded room each morning, while the nurse made her bed, and each morning she ran to me and hit me on the head with my own slipper. It had a hard heel, but it was the unexpectedness more than the bang which annoyed me. When she did this for three mornings running, I began to think she fancied I was a gong or some other idiotic nonsense! I decided to do something about this perfunctory tap on my head each morning. I was forced to solve the problem myself, and the practice was discontinued. It was a simple solution. I hid my slippers under my mattress. I remained there in the Hold another day, two – and still I was not asked to go back to Long Trench. I worried continually, and I was indecisive and apathetic. Alternatively I remembered to 'have faith' and prayed fervently for Mother's recovery.

Chapter 17

A day later, Delia arrived, or, rather, was pushed through the passage door, which was then slammed in her face and locked. I discovered by degrees that the nurses and patients alike were afraid of her.

It was a matter of principle this time. It had been suggested to her by a psychiatrist that she should take a course of insulin shock or ECT treatment. He also promised to send her home afterwards. Delia was no fool, and never mixed hypothesis with probability. When high, she was either put into a detention room in Prospect House, her accepted abode, or sent to the Hold, where she was now. In Prospect House she had broken the lock of the detention room door by using her iron bedstead as a battering ram. The lock had to be repaired, and meantime Delia was sent to the Hold to prevent further depredations beyond.

I noticed the two seasoned nurses grinning at each other knowingly. The senior of the two called to her.

'Hello Delia!'

Delia turned her back on the locked door, gave the two nurses a contemptuous look, and then proceeded to ignore them. She walked slowly, deliberately, up and down the aisles between the beds. She peered into the whitewashed cell, which, unlike the padded cell, had a peep-hole in the door. She gave a deliberate sort of high-pitched yelp.

'That's right, damn you, leave the poor devil inside to freeze to death without a stitch of clothes.'

She faced the nurses now, and I could see her eyes were bloodshot, but her face was pale.

'Sonia's always in there,' she shouted, 'it's not fair. There's worse than her here. You there!' She addressed me. 'What the devil are you doing here?'

She swung her long flaxen blonde hair around her shoulders as if it were a cat-o'-nine-tails. She rounded on the nurses again.

'Haven't you enough here to swab the decks without bringing down . . . this . . .' and she indicated me vaguely. She wandered about then, with a deliberate, measured gait, as if looking for someone to attack.

The nurses finally pacified her, and invited her to take a cup of tea with them. She grudgingly accepted, as if conferring a favour. After tea, she demanded to be bedded in a quiet place, and chose the bed on the other side of the fire. The poor evicted patient was made to get up then and dress, and she was called for by a nurse from Prospect House. She was told briefly that she would remain in Prospect House until Delia's return. This arrangement is unofficially called 'the swop'. It is a very complicated procedure, but it is facilitated when both patients are willing. The nurses put Delia into the freshly made bed and gave her a sedative. After a few minutes of leonine behaviour she appeared to doze off. Rosie came to visit me. She apologised, saying she could only stay a few minutes.

'Look who's here,' I said, pointing to Delia.

Rosie put her fingers to her lips with a cautious gesture. 'Shush! I don't want her to see me, in her mood.'

'Why, Rosie, doesn't she work with you in the laundry?'

'Work! She stays two hours, and she gets paid for that, for "doing" for the nurses. She gets more for those two hours than I can earn in a week. She has an advantage, with her full parole, she goes back and forth to the nurses' home. There's extra for collection and delivery, you see.' Rosie carefully scrutinised me. 'It's unofficial of course, not a word!'

'Well, that's no reason to fall out,' I said.

'When she gets high she can be very insulting,' Rosie said bitterly. 'You often heard, Honor, the saying that "a little knowledge is a dangerous thing"?'

'Yes.'

'Well, Delia picks up a lot of big words. She hears the nurses talking, and she reads their books, that they study for their exams. Do you want to hear what she said to me?'

'Is it the truth?'

'Of course not, but people who heard her say it to me will think it is.'

'Just what did she accuse you of, Rosie?'

'She said I was . . . a dissipated old schizophrenic!'

'Good heavens, what did she mean?'

'Well, whatever it is, she shouted it at me in the laundry, and everybody laughing at their own ignorance. And all because I would not lend her my soap. She can be very trifling.' Rosie sniffed.

A voice shouted across. It was Delia, alert.

'You! Who told you to come here, Rosie Posy. I'll complain to the doctor, you so-and-so . . .'

She got up on one elbow.

'You know you shouldn't be here, definite . . . ly not. No visitors allowed here.'

Rosie got up to go.

'There you are,' she said quietly to me. 'And in a few days' time you would think butter wouldn't melt in her mouth.'

The nurse came over to Rosie and me.

'Rosie, please, will you go, another scene with Delia would just about finish me, I'm exhausted.'

'All right, all right, nurse, I'm going. Goodbye Honor darlin', I'll come again another time.' She nodded disapprovingly at Delia's back. 'She never stays long.'

Delia had dozed off again, but Rosie left in a hurry.

It was Sunday again, the day Mother used to visit me, so very long ago it seemed now. I was told I could get up and go to church. I had continually prayed for Mother since she entered hospital and she was always in my heart. I dressed, and a nurse explained that afterwards I would have to return to bed, as they had yet to ask the doctor for permission for me to leave the Hold and return to Long Trench. They promised to ask her on the following Monday morning. I nodded, for I had been there long enough, I thought.

I put on my old brown coat and beret, and I went to church with a mixed group of patients from three or four divisions. Some I recognised from Long Trench. I resolved not to ask God for my liberty this Sunday, but to ask for Mother's health instead.

Afterwards we gathered outside to be segregated and counted before returning to our respective buildings. Matron was standing outside the church. The white nylon veil was blown by the breeze, around and about the collar of her tweed coat. She called to me gently.

'Honor, please wait, I want to talk to you.'

I was surprised, for it was unusual. She walked up to me. She was a widow and she had taken up her profession again when her husband died. She was very tall, a handsome woman, with steel-grey wavy hair showing beneath her billowing veil.

'Yes, Matron,' I said.

'Honor I have sad news for you.'

My heart sank and an old ache tugged.

'Is it Mother, Matron?'

'Yes, dear. I am sorry to have to tell you she died this morning at 2am in hospital.'

Matron gently took my arm, and led me towards the patients and nurses who were waiting for me. 'You may take your patients back, Nurse. I will take Honor back myself.'

Obediently they walked on ahead of us. I was grieving silently, and I felt very lonely, but not frightened. That came later. My thoughts were that Mother would not, could not, come, no more, to see me. The sense of loss, of pain, my thoughts stopped there, as if that was all, but it was more than enough, it was all I could bear. I was beginning to lose the most precious things of life, and I did not comprehend fully, for then, consciously, I was not aware even of my loss, but, subconsciously, aware that I was being cheated. I would never lose anything carelessly, indifferently, no. Mother must have died because I was not there to exhort her to live. Matron's comforting presence failed to relieve me. She had her arm through mine, and she walked slowly with me, talking – gentle words, comforting words.

'Your mother would not like to see you distressed, Honor. She is happy now, in heaven, and she would want you to be happy too.'

'I know, Matron, but I loved her, and I feel she would not have died if I had been there, to tell her, at least to make her happy, and see her happy, before she went . . .'

I broke off here and began to cry again.

'Your aunty phoned, Honor,' Matron said. 'Your brother is home and taking care of all the arrangements.'

'My brother,' I said stupidly. 'Mother, who was with her when . . . did she ask for me?'

'Your aunty told me on the phone to tell you she will come up to see you after the funeral tomorrow. She was with your mother for a short time yesterday evening, and your brother, of course, he was there.'

'Mother always preferred me. She, she said I was the only one who understood her,' I said pathetically. 'I should have been there.'

'It is God's will,' Matron said. 'We only heard this morning. Now, Honor, don't grieve.'

I began to sob again, and she handed me a fresh handkerchief. I suddenly wanted to see my brother Paul and my aunt.

'Matron, do you think, could you phone them, I want to go to the funeral.'

'I'm afraid that is impossible dear,' she shook her head sadly. 'The superintendent thinks it would be unwise for you to go. He cannot take the responsibility. There is nothing we can do, Honor, you understand, don't you, dear? Our hands are tied.'

I heaved silently, vainly trying to control the sobs and my heavy, aching heart.

Chapter 18

We arrived back at Long Trench after what seemed eternity. I heard Matron say to the first nurse we met to put me back to bed, to give me a warm drink of milk and a sedative. I went below and obediently undressed, drank the hot milk with the sedative, and got into my bed.

I lay passively inert all day, accepting mechanically tea and hot drinks, but my mind and I were far away, in lush green fields of childhood memories. I was not now in the infamous Hold of the Big House, no, I was back at home, talking to Mother.

She was smiling as always, the same poignant, sad smile, an expression on her face of ineffable sweetness and tenderness. She was combing my hair, caressing and combing. 'Poor little craytur,' she would say, to my delight, meanwhile stroking my hair.

'Mammy,' I insisted on attention, for I had determined to find out, somehow, 'How was I born? Where did I come from?'

She answered my question, still smiling, caressing, amused. 'Why, under a head of cabbage, dear.'

I remember I fell into a wondering silence, pondering her words. I felt that this was not usual, that very few children, if any, could have been born there – under a head of cabbage.

'Mammy,' I said, 'do you mean it, under a real head of cabbage?'

'Yes, dear,' she said, softly, mysteriously.

The book was open, and my eyes were glued to pages of memory, my mind too, speeding from scene to scene. I could never penetrate the mystery of the beautiful stories she told, in her lovely voice, stories so fantastic and lovely that I shall always remember them.

Her diary, I meant to take it with me, it was now at home, locked in the piano. It was the last place I saw it, and it was dedicated to me. The writing was small and perfect, but difficult to fathom. I remembered reading a few lines when I was fifteen – the time I fell in love – but I began to cry after a few pages. It was sad, and I could not bear it. Sadness – past, present, and now, future.

The photo was nice, Mother and myself, the baby. The baby was lying in a cot, chuckling, laughing, kicking delightedly with chubby legs, reaching up chubby little hands to Mother, who leaned over the cot with old-fashioned grace and dignity and tenderness.

I started nervously. The doctor was at my bedside.

'How are you, Honor? Did you give her a sedative, Nurse? Eating? No?'

'Doctor, I feel terrible. I can't eat. It was a big shock.'

'I am sorry, Honor. Please accept my condolences. Be brave, there's a good girl. Take a good rest and tomorrow you can go down to the waiting room and see your aunty.'

'Is Paul, my brother, coming?'

'I don't know, Honor. He is taking care of the funeral arrangements. He may have to go back to work.'

'May I go to the funeral, Doctor?'

'I don't think so, Honor. The superintendent thinks it is not necessary.'

'Mammy, please play something.'

I would sit on the little varnished piano stool, like a gnome, and Mother would thump the yellow and black keys with her dainty, plump fingers – 'The Minstrel Boy to the War has Gone'. I would join in in my soprano. She would hear hymns now. Her friends told her once that she was like a popular new film star. I found a picture of the famous actress in a book and compared her with Mammy's photo. Yes, there was a resemblance. But Mother was not an actress; her daily fictions, or roles, were not professional but the whole invention of a loving mother.

When we became poor, she had few clothes, for she was a widow. I hated black, the men with the black top hats who took

Daddy away. They left a big black crepe bow on the knocker of the hall door, and they never walked on the sawdust in the shop, but ate it, on the ham, at the long table. They were so many black top hats, black-suited shadows, and they came back again in every nightmare.

That was long ago. I was five and Mother twenty-five. Black clothes meant sadness, but Mother wore little white piqué collars and cuffs. When I was sixteen, she wore navy. She seemed to suffer all alone, and I suffered for her secretly, silently. I would sit hunched up in the squashed chamber of my heart, worrying, desperately anxious to help, but unable to do so. She was always selling or renting something. In the beginning it was always something big, like Monks Island, on the river at home. She had inherited it, and she sold it for a song when Father died. To pay death duties, she said. A hundred pounds for a hundred acres, today it sounds fantastic, but Mother was satisfied. What use was a lonely hermitage to her? Alas, her furs went also, and the best silver, which used to be in the red velvet box in the best mahogany wardrobe. When the wardrobe was sold, among other things, life became very austere indeed.

The times the electricity was cut off, for instance. I hated the tallow candles we had to use, not because of the candles, but because the once brightly lit big corner house was conspicuously plunged in gloom, and my friends at school asked me next day what all the candles were for, and I could not explain. I smile sadly now, at the futility of it all. Daddy was not insured, Mother was not insured, and I suppose that is why Paul sold the house so soon.

The Hold was hubbub, and I began to feel restless. I sat up in my bed, weary and tear-stained. The patients had not come near me. They seemed to know by instinct that I wanted to be alone in my grief. The nurse handed out two huge slices of bread and butter from an enamel tray. I had not realised how hungry I was. The night nurses came on duty, and they sympathised with me. They offered me some of their own supper, which I refused, but I accepted a mug of hot milk and a sedative gratefully, and fell into a dreamless sleep soon after that.

My thoughts were very sad next morning. Now that Mother was dead, there was nothing really to look forward to – no home, no letters, no visitors, except the perfunctory duty call from the odd relative, no parcels, and – no liberty. I did not expect Aunty until five o'clock, but I rose early and washed and dressed. I asked Matron if I could go to the chapel to pray for Mother. It was all I could do now.

The Big Boss came down to see me. She expressed her condolences uncouthly and I knew by her manner that she did not really care. She said my aunty had sent a message to say it would be after five when she arrived. I thanked her listlessly. The day dragged on.

Aunty was alone when the nurse escorted me to the visitors' room. Her taxi was outside – waiting. She was plumper and smaller than Mother, and also very prim and proper, as aunties should be. Questions tumbled from my lips.

'Mother, did she ask for me?'

'Oh yes.'

'I wanted to go to the funeral. If you had asked me I'm sure they would have let me go,' I said reproachfully.

'There was no time, Honor. I had to go home to the children, phone the hospital here, and arrange the funeral details with Paul. We have been going all the time since yesterday.'

'I see,' I said dully; I did not see at all.

'Why has Paul not written or come up to see me?' I asked.

'It was not necessary. I believe your Mother wanted to save him the expense. It would cost him five pounds each time, to visit you. In his work it is impracticable, and it is too long a journey.'

'He is selling the house?'

'Yes, there is an offer. He got an advance for the funeral expenses. I was surprised your mother was not insured.'

'Mother never planned far ahead.'

'You were crying, Honor?'

'Yes. I am dried up now. Aunty,' I pleaded, 'what is going to happen to me now? I was nearly ready to leave.'

'Well, dear, I can't say. Tom's sister is staying with us, and even if they allowed me to take you out, I have nowhere to put you up.'

'What does Paul say?'

'What can he do? He is staying in digs, near his work. He is engaged to be married, did you know?'

'No. He never writes.'

Aunty rose to her feet.

'I took you up some clothes, some of mine, you can renovate them, and here's a cake and some fruit. Honor, I must go, dear, I have a long journey home, and work tomorrow. I will write and tell you the news.'

I was escorted back to the Hold. Death had struck twice. Mother had gone and now, what was to be my fate – a living death? Some instinct within me, undefined, made me suddenly angry. I wanted to confront the enemy, the monstrous, spider-like, invisible, living malice that inveigles you into a parlour to be cowed and enslaved. My father and mother were dead, but that was no reason to leave me in a mental hospital – and – indefinitely. I would soon become another dependant in the Legion of the Lost, unless – I thought – I must insist somehow on my liberty, or else I would become a life prisoner. I had been told that I could go. Now, I could not go. Why? Madness? But whose?

Chapter 19

'No, we could have starved, for all my relatives cared. Mother often denied herself food, to give to us. Times were very hard after Father died. Desperate sometimes. We got a bare subsistence from renting parts of the house.'

'Poor Honor, 'tis a sad enough story.'

'I was nursing and I lost the vocation, Rosie. I resigned, although Mother wished me to have some profession, and that cost nothing. I thought of her all the time, alone, poor, and perhaps ill, so I went home to be with her. I had no sense then, Rosie, I should have finished I suppose. I thought I would get a job at home, but I became ill with worry. I think Mother must have told everybody at home that I had qualified or that I was home on holidays, all for the present, you know Rosie, but expedient to Mother, of that I am sure. I became ill with worry, and the family doctor advised Mother to put me in here, for a rest. It was free, you see, Rosie,' I said bitterly.

'I see, darlin'. God help us all, 'tis a hard world. But pray, darlin', maybe your brother will take you out.'

I rose wearily, for I was mentally and physically exhausted.

'Good night Rosie. You are very kind to listen. I've hardly spoken for days.'

I slept, and without sedatives, for I had been transferred from the Hold back to Long Trench, to a different room, and I was beside a dormitory now; the walls were thicker and the sounds I heard were not stupidly repetitive. I did not mind the occasional shouts and cries in the night.

The week passed quietly, and I went about quietly, dusting a little, polishing a little, and walking outdoors a little on the walks. Sometimes I chatted to Oonagh, or Rosie, Kathleen, Bessie and many others. I became acquainted with many of the patients. About five or six days after the funeral I had two letters. One was from Aunty, the other was from Paul.

I read Paul's letter. It was a cool letter, one you would write to a stranger, or a very low-IQ person. There was no acknowledgement, reference even, no human understanding of my circumstances in his letter. The usual expressions of sympathy were conspicuously absent. He said that as he was working so far away he could not visit me. He had sold the house, but he did not say for how much. He hinted he would have to marry, as he and his fiancée had romantically agreed marriage would be less expensive than digs. Very little else was added. The selfish contents of this heartless document gave me a depressed nausea. I tore it up. I was left now in no doubt that he did not intend to take me out, and that, as far as he was concerned, I had ceased to exist except as a possible liability which he would definitely not incur.

Spring came, and suddenly anywhere seemed preferable to Long Trench and the Big Boss. I decided to go to work in the sewing room. Matron said I could start on the morrow.

The sewing room had a sociable atmosphere. Talking was not encouraged. Nurse Best was in charge there, and she tried to make life more pleasant for us. She was a kind, tolerant person, but she insisted on the patients' attention to work primarily. It was all soulless utilitarian work. The clothes each patient wore were made here by other patients. Nurse Best gave me a needle, a spool of white thread, a thimble and a cut-out cotton chemise to sew.

The first person to introduce herself was Miss Lovelost. I had seen her before, at the dance, but I had not spoken to her. She was very old, but spare and alert. She sat very straight on her chair, and there was a perpetual pleased smile on her face, a little-girl smile, that began in the eyes and went down to her tiny prim mouth and back again, in the way sunlight beams and diminishes on earthy water. She lived in the immediate present and never suggested she had any adult memories. She greeted me with a funny, long-toothed smile, and a little old-fashioned curtsy.

'How do you do, Miss Honor,' she said.

She went over to Nurse Best and sat beside her, still looking over at me with that tiny smile.

'She's nice. Hum! Hum! I think she will do very nicely, thank you.'

Nurse Best playfully and affectionately pinched her cheek.

'What do you mean, she'll do? Of course she will do, you silly old goose!'

'You know best, dear,' said Miss Lovelost.

We chuckled at what we thought was Miss Lovelost's wit, and Nurse Best smiled, as if she knew something about Miss Lovelost which we did not.

I made four chemises, sometimes five, per day, when I worked there, for almost four years. I was a quick worker, and sometimes I knitted a cardigan for a change, but I was satisfied with sewing chemises. Nurse Best cut out twenty at a time en masse. When they were new, they were stiff, wide and bulky, but when the washing machine finished with them, they clung to the figure. Occasionally, shrouds were made there, by machine. Some patients hand-sewed flannelette night-dresses, and men's night-shirts, and shirts, and these had to be finished by machine. I sewed many of these, also, by hand. There were five sewing machines there, and one huge, unvarnished cutting-out table in the centre. There was a smaller table further back, near a window. There was a food and crockery cupboard beside that. Inside the cupboard, on shelves, was bread and butter, tea and sugar, a huge enamelled teapot and mugs, all of which were used for the patients' elevenses.

Weeks, months, years passed. Four Christmases more were celebrated and still I had no offer of freedom. I received the usual duty cards, and the occasional duty parcel with letter. I wrote begging letters to every relative I could think of, pleading with them to take me out, just for a week, so that I could have an address and reference, to apply for a job outside. The few letters I did receive in return were not replies to my request. They were carefully, coldly worded letters, ignoring completely my pleas. They wrote of their own trivial domestic cares, pretending they were major crises, for twenty years. For twenty years, I was informed occasionally of these domestic crises, their worldly progress, and their ambitions. Especially their ambitions.

Still I persevered with the letters, determined somehow to cheat the system and cheat it of its prey, this soulless machine of a place. My bitterness at my detention would greatly increase when I thought that they knew I was well, and Paul knew also, for the superintendent, on my request, had written to this effect and told him he could claim me out any time. Paul had not replied. If he had come to see me even then, after the first five, or ten unnecessary years there, I would have forgiven him, but he preferred to leave me in forever, where insanity, on such a long detention, is assumed or presupposed. Legally, I could do nothing, and legally, the outside had the upper hand. In such moments of despair and impotent fury, I prayed. I prayed until peace and tranquillity returned.

There was always work, of course. Sewing did not appeal to me as a full-time occupation, but here, at least, I was safe from the 'Ogress' of Long Trench. I think the Ogress really is a more emotionally descriptive name for the Big Boss of Long Trench. It was a word that had different shades of meaning. I called her the Ogress, for after all, she was not really my boss any more. I worked under Nurse Best's management now, I assured myself. So from then on, she was the Ogress. I wondered what other names she was given privately by her charges.

Chapter 20

Years passed. One bank holiday Monday, I had a free day. There was no sewing room work that day. There was nothing to look forward to except a promised walk after lunch for us all, weather permitting.

I was sitting in Long Trench, near the office. I thought of my blue linen and silk pyjamas in my case, probably still on a shelf inside that office. I decided to ask the Ogress for them. It was a bank holiday, things were slack, she could hardly refuse. I knocked quietly on the door. The Ogress was discussing some unknown patient's 'diminishing responsibility'. I knocked again, louder.

'Yes, what is it, come in.'

Then there was an unflattering remark about pests. I went in warily, not sure of my reception. The place was cloudy with smoke.

'Oh it's you!'

She looked significantly at her deputy.

'Monica, take a look around outside, the rounds haven't gone yet.'

The deputy left, and the Ogress lit a fresh cigarette.

'I suppose you want to go home,' she said with studied sarcasm.

'Would you please let me have my pyjamas, they are in my case, I may as well wear them,' I said quickly, ignoring her remark. She flicked ash off her cigarette irritably.

'You will have to wear what everybody else wears. You come here and bother me, to get you some mouldy old garment that's probably moth-eaten by now. Well you can't have it.' She stubbed her cigarette out viciously. 'Now get out, get out.'

And she caught me by the shoulder, spun me round towards the door and roughly pushed me out of the office. I stood outside, dazed, immovable, liquid fire swimming in my eyes, blazing and darting, trying to leap out, my fists clenched fiercely to my sides. It was all I could do to restrain myself from going back in and – pushing her into her plush chair.

Suddenly I noticed a small bottle of white tablets on the window ledge. I walked over and picked it up. Yes, it was a small bottle of Luminal tablets, frequently given for sedation. I slipped it into my pocket on impulse. I felt a pleasurable yet grim sense of power as I deliberately walked down the Long Trench away from her office. I thought, here is a weapon against her . . . I find now in my possession about one hundred Luminal tablets, which, in the event of torture, would be release from this oppressive den and its presiding Ogress. I felt the cool glass of the bottle again and smiled grimly. This would probably be the only opportunity I would ever have here again. I had the direct, simplest means of escape at hand. I walked on, automatically, towards the toilets, a place where some patients hid for hours, sometimes all day, if they were not missed between meals and counts.

I turned suddenly, and walked back. My mind was cooler, critical and analytical again. I went and sat on my chair. She was not worth it. The Ogress, and the unexpected means of revenge, receded into relative insignificance. I thought, I must get rid of the tablets at once. I waited until I was sure nobody had noticed me. I stepped quickly onto the chair, and dropped the tablets through the narrow air slot, halfway up the window, onto the grassy earth below. They fell outside. I was safe, at least from suicide.

The Ogress emerged from her office cell and threw my blue pyjamas at me. 'There they are, and don't let me or the patients see you going about in them without your dressing gown. Understand?' she roared.

They were damp and crushed, but they were so familiar . . . mine. Mother had bought them for me. 'Oh yes, of course, thank you. I must keep them in good condition, for going out . . . home . . .'

I faltered here. I had no home now. My home was no more. Strangers lived there now. A cruel, almost vindictive expression came into her eyes.

'You will never go home,' she rasped. 'You have no home. Nobody wants you.'

She stopped and waited for the effect of her words.

'I am not insane. The doctor has written to my relatives saying I am fit and well, and I can go when they claim me.'

'They don't want you, and the longer you're here, the longer they will leave you. For ever.'

'I will get out, you'll see. There is such a thing as justice. I will.'

'No.'

She repeated this with an obvious sadistic delight, revelling, yet hypocritically shaking her head dolefully, negatively.

'Yes,' I said.

'No,' she repeated in the same way.

My heart constricted. I felt like the pendulum of an ancient clock, that had been grabbed and sent whizzing madly by a vandal's hand. The hot tears trickled down my cheeks. If only I had not thrown away those tablets . . . I raised my hand, sudden rage blinding me to the consequences, and smashed it through the narrow, sturdy little pane of glass, one of the many of the barred window beside me.

I felt no pain, I was so enraged. I still looked at her, questioning, entreaty for justice, compassion, behind my tears, challenging, daring her to say I had no hope, my hand still raised.

The mask at last had dropped from her face. It was no longer provocative, and ignorant. It was malevolent, satisfied.

'Now you'll never get out at all.'

She called a nurse who was hurrying to the scene.

'I will, you'll see, I will,' I said, and smashed my bleeding hand through another pain of glass. I was still unconscious of the physical pain, although my hand was now a crimson, glass-stuck horror.

I was taken, crying, to the surgery by the nurse. The sheet draped around my hand was already a crimson boxing glove. At the surgery, the doctor removed the pieces of glass, and washed and dressed my hand with a medical preparation.

When he finished, it was double its size because of all the cotton wool.

I began to imagine the Ogress, back in Long Trench writing her report, her own version of my 'destructive mania'. I thought miserably: Now I've done it. I can't go to work now, and it will be worse now, much worse. It was. The matron had been told of my 'evil deed'. The Ogress had of course written her own version of what happened – I had rebelled against my lot. I am quite certain her report was prejudiced. I was not asked by the doctors, or Matron, for my account of the incident. Whatever the Ogress did write, that report got me five years' detention in the Hold.

During those five years, I often prayed for a firing squad, something quick and clean anyway. I was allowed out of bed, but only just, to the toilet and to the weekly bath. I was kept under constant supervision. I was now considered unpredictable and a danger to smug officialdom.

A year after I went there, I saw my face in a night nurse's mirror. There were no mirrors in the Hold. How strange my face was, so different. My eyes were sorrowful, with dark irises, and I used to have gay, laughing eyes. The days and months passed wearily, until one day I noticed that my healed hand was different to the other. The cuts had healed, but a tendon projected awkwardly in the palm of my hand. It had contracted and the hand was odd looking. I began to feel restless, which feeling soon changed to recklessness. A ludicrous plan formed in my imaginative brain.

I picked a nice quiet afternoon, after lunch, when even the eccentrics are in need of a 'siesta'. I slipped on my dressing gown. It was faded now, and I knew it would soon be taken from me, as it had been washed six or seven times in the laundry, and would soon be of no practical use. I walked out to the toilets, which were at the end of the dormitory, behind a corner. I went into the fourth and last toilet. They had no doors. I stood up on the toilet basin, balancing precariously, tied one end of my dressing gown cord to the water lever fixture above and tied the other end around my neck.

'Now,' I thought, 'all I have to do is jump off.'

There was a sudden yell from one of the patients. I just caught a glimpse of a white-faced patient, fleeing in terror. 'Nurse! Nurse! Come quickly! The toilet – Honor is hanging herself in the toilet!'

I looked as guilty and frustrated as I could manage in such an awkward position, a thin, odd-looking figure wobbling on a lavatory basin. They untied me from the gibbet and spoke kind and gentle words to me as they untied the cord from around my neck. I suffered all their ministrations in silence, with an apparently inscrutable detachment. Matron was sent for.

'Honor, you were a very naughty girl. Trying to hang yourself! You know, dear, that is a dreadful thing to try.'

I put on an act then, and said, with as much incoherence as I could simulate: 'Try? But I did. It's all over.'

Matron looked baffled, or so I thought. She told the nurses as she left to prepare to give me paraldehyde.

At last there was to be a break in the infernal boredom. Now I was to know what the magic potion was. I had seen too much fuss about taking it to waste time pretending. I took it unprotesting, and immediately I was away from the Hold. I was going somewhere, effortlessly, unhampered. I was free, like a disembodied spirit, yet human, struggling, trying to stabilise the passing moments, failing, slipping . . . Afterwards, nobody mentioned the hanging episode to me, so I suppose the unforgettable paraldehyde was intended to make me forget about it. I noticed, too, that my dressing gown disappeared, and I never saw it again. It was probably used as a floor polisher, as is done with all the worn-out garments in the Big House.

Chapter 21

I remained in the Hold for five years, unrevised. On the fifth anniversary of my internment there, the psychiatrist came and interviewed me in bed. If I promised to be good, I could go back to Long Trench. I would have to work in the sewing room again. She had written to my aunty, in the absence of my mother, and Aunty had agreed that I should have ECT treatment.

I shivered involuntarily at the thought of past scenes of ECT in the admission block, but I agreed to do all she said, otherwise, I was led to believe, I would have been kept in the Hold indefinitely. She was quite pleased with my response, and before she departed, she said that the treatment would not be immediately – but soon.

The next day I was released. I squeezed through the partly opened door, held so by one nurse, while another nurse tried to keep back the 'iglooist', who was getting bored and had decided on a 'slip through'. The door was banged and I was alone, outside and free. I was dressed in Aunty's jersey suit. I walked up the passage, rather unsteadily, to Long Trench. The first person I met was Rosie, all smiles, offering me snuff, which I refused, and a mug of strong tea she had brewed herself. We sat in our old place on the couch.

'I wanted to visit you, Honor darlin', but the villains would not admit me. They said you were not fit for visitors. Did you have a bad time?'

'Do you know, Rosie, I am not the same person at all. Is she still here?'

'The Ogress? No, thank God. She went on sick leave first, then she applied for a transfer a year ago. She is in Sunset House.'

'And as you say, Rosie, "may all bad luck go with her!" Who is in charge here now?'

'Aha, a very nice lady – Nurse Best. She got tired of the sewing room. There was a change all round, you might say.'

'Oh, I'm glad Rosie. I like her, she's kind and understanding.'

'Indeed she is.'

'Rosie, I'm thinking of going to the laundry. There is more freedom there, more walking about, more air. What's the charge nurse there like?'

'A very nice nurse. I'll mention it to her this afternoon – I have to go there now. I'm owed a few bob.'

'All right, Rosie. See you this evening.'

I walked down to the fireguard. Oonagh was there, the same Oonagh, fiercer looking, though, and her eyebrows seemed to bristle. I sat down on a chair near her.

'You hurted your hand, dear.'

She spoke as if the last five years had never been, as if what had happened had just happened in the present.

'The ratepayers will sue me, Oonagh, I banged it on a window.' I curled my lips, trying to match her mouth as it curled contemptuously. 'A nurse and I had an argument. I just did it for . . . emphasis,' I replied, trying to imitate her now superior smile.

'She persecuted me too, dear. She has dreadful big feet.'

Here, Oonagh tapped daintily with her toe, an exultant little tap-dance, but only for a few seconds. 'One day, dear, after you went down, she ordered a nurse to cut my hair. She was jealous of it, you know. But she didn't succeed.'

I gathered the details later, from Rosie.

Eagle-like, Oonagh had attacked. It was a verbal swoop; words and incitements were her weapons. She reminded everybody in Long Trench, for one whole day, of the threatened danger. All day, her shrill, derisive voice jeered and sneered at the staff. She reminded each patient of her miserable lot. She referred to the jollop and the cascara as 'their only treatment'. She reminded many patients of wrongs they had brooded over for twenty years or more. She talked about Sunset House, the cul-de-sac, the blind alley, she called it, the crowded inn for the unclaimed and the aged, the blind alley, she insisted again, which now harboured, in disgrace, the old loyal comrades and veterans of the past – heroes of victorious guerrilla wars and vendettas.

She kept the Ogress so busy for days that she completely forgot Oonagh's dark locks. Rosie claimed she had excited the patients in an 'uncanny' manner. It was bedlam. Basins of paraffin, with combs, were overturned and spilt, chairs were banged, spade fashion, up and down Long Trench, until the legs fell off, and the carpenter and Ice-Blue were swamped with legless chairs to repair. Spoons, knives, forks, vanished mysteriously. The Ogress counted cutlery until, I would say, a wooden spoon was all the paradise she asked. The rebellion waxed outside also. The patients were not allowed out on their walks until the Ogress had frisked each one at the door for a missing spoon or fork. The patients, losing all patience at the delays and insinuations, at last broke out into open rebellion. They broke away from the crocodile files, and ran whooping across the playing fields into the forbidden territory of the men's habitations. The Ogress, herself a charge nurse, had to run across the playing fields and assist her limited staff in the round-up.

The reprisals provoked by the uncanny power of Oonagh continued until the Ogress, driven nearly out of her mind, to use her own hackneyed expression, sent in a doctor's certificate and went on sick leave, and then finally moved to Sunset House.

Nurse Best was nice to me. In fact I am inclined to think that it was she who had used her influence to have me reinstated again in Long Trench.

She came over to where I was sitting, beside Oonagh, and shook my hand.

'I am glad to see you well again, Honor. I am charge nurse here now. Do you like the idea?'

'Oh yes indeed, Nurse Best. In fact I have decided now to go to work again. The laundry, not the sewing room.'

'That's good, Honor. Would you like to wait until after your

ECT treatment? I think you're having your first shock tomorrow.'

ECT. I had forgotten.

'How long will it take?'

'Oh, about three weeks altogether, eighteen shocks. You will be brought over to admission each morning after breakfast, and be brought back afterwards, about eleven o'clock.'

'I am to go tomorrow morning, so soon?' I asked in dismay.

'Cheer up, Honor, it's not too bad, you know.' She was about to leave when she added, casually: 'Honor, I have put you in a quiet room near the night nurses' kitchen. Would you prefer a dormitory? I could move somebody out to the room, if you wish.'

'Oh no, Nurse, thank you. The room will do fine. I dislike snoring.'

'Very well, Honor. First thing in the morning, then, treatment. No breakfast for you, of course, just a cup of tea. They will give you your breakfast in the admission when you wake up. I shall send a nurse over for you.'

Rosie had news for me that evening. She beckoned me to sit beside her on the couch. Nurse Goodson had said she would be very pleased to have me work in the laundry.

'She is a kind, motherly person, Honor, but "there's no rose without a thorn".'

'Do you mean she can be nasty?'

'Ah, no, not at all, dear. It's just that sometimes she can be bitter, not offensive, just – bitter.'

'Well, please thank her for me, Rosie, but I regret I can't go for another three weeks. Nurse Best is sending me for eighteen shock treatments, ECT. She says I may go to the laundry when the course is over.'

'Good heavens, child, what do they want to do that for?'

'I have gone through so much now, Rosie, that I don't care. It is about the only treatment I have not had, and they can't do any more then, can they?' I gave her an affectionate hug. 'We will have great chats when I am working with you in the laundry.'

'Aye, that's right, Honor, and I can put a few bob in your way, too. Nurses, the young 'uns, dance mad, man mad, sometimes I haven't time to do all their things. They would pay you, Honor, to iron their dance frocks. It would be pocket money for you. Of course, Delia is a gangster, you know. She gets double money out of them, for half the work I do. They're afraid of her, and she demands the pay in advance.'

'Thank you, Rosie, you are kind. I have to go to bed early tonight, to be bright and ready tomorrow for the treatment, so I'll say goodnight, Rosie.'

I slept well, in my new quiet cell. Nurse Best had found my cream silk and lace pyjamas, had them aired for me, and gave them to me without a word. It made me feel very civilised, and I fell asleep immediately.

Chapter 22

Next morning I set out for the admission escorted by Nurse Benny. She was of a placid, bovine disposition, with a fixed smile of good nature on her chubby face. The morning air was chilly, and I had on over Aunty's jersey suit my winter coat, slung over my shoulders, cloak fashion. We went on a circuitous route, past Sunset House. Nurse Best had given Nurse Benny her orders to go this way so that I would benefit from the walk and fresh air. I felt nervous, and a feeling of butterflies was in my stomach; a sudden fear developed of the unknown ordeal before me. I cannot go through with it, I thought wildly, I just cannot. I gave no indication of my wild thoughts to Nurse Benny, who plodded stoically beside me. There was an old wall overlooking the thoroughfare outside, just opposite Sunset House. It was hand-built, from loose stones, and some jutted out, making ideal foot-holds. When we were about six yards from it, on a wild, mad impulse, I swung off my coat, and threw it over the nurse's head, and made a mad dash for the wall. I was halfway up when I felt strong, firm hands pulling me down by my feet. It was Nurse Benny, indignant, fierce, and surprised at the totally unexpected. I reluctantly descended to the ground.

'I do not want ECT, Nurse. I hate it. I hate you all.'

She took my arm persuasively.

'Now, come on, Honor, please, there's a good girl.'

I slung the coat again about my shoulders, and two docile individuals, to all appearances, arrived at the admission block. A group of patients stared at us through the windows as we approached. I continued on down to the locker room to change, while Nurse Benny went into the charge nurse's office to tell her of my attempt to climb the wall.

I undressed in the locker room and put on the nightdress a nurse handed me. The charge nurse came to see me. I expected her.

'You are to go in first, Honor,' she said, sternly. 'Doctor's orders. We don't want you getting nerves again.'

'How many more are there for it?' I asked.

'Just three today. Now come on down to the dormitory. The doctor will be here in a few minutes.'

I followed her, through the large admission ward, into the middle dormitory, where the 'theatre' was screened off. It was exactly as I remembered it. The 'operation bed' on its own, two more beds ready and made up appropriately. The bed was reversed, for the foot was now to accommodate the head of the person to be treated. On one of the tables were bowls, swabs, drums and other incidental implements. One bowl was half-full of saline, one contained swabs, and the other was empty. Another small table was beside the electric plug-fitting, to accommodate the electric apparatus. I stood beside the bed, waiting. Two nurses stood there, waiting. The doctor arrived, jauntily, on time, about ten o'clock. He addressed me breezily.

'Haha, Honor, heard you tried to escape.'

'No luck,' I said dourly.

He laughed and took his electric machine from the little black case.

'You don't like ECT, is that it?'

I did not care to confuse or antagonise this 'electrician', who was not infallible, and might inadvertently become my executioner.

'I don't mind now. I have never had this treatment before, Doctor.'

The nurse signalled me to remove my shoes and to jump up on the bed.

'There is nothing to be afraid of Honor,' he said, as he tested and clicked his machine.

He was behind me now, but from the corner of my eyes I could see him adjusting some contraption around his own head. My two temples were swabbed with saline, and the 'apparatus' was strapped around my head.

'Ready, Nurses?'

'Yes, Doctor,' they said in unison.

Two nurses, one on each side, held me by each shoulder, and the third nurse held my two feet together. This was done to prevent me struggling during the treatment. I had no intention of moving a muscle. If I move, I thought, I might fuse the whole damn thing. I submitted tamely and passively to the entire operation. More clicking of switches, and he said again, 'Ready.'

The nurses' grips tightened, and he switched on.

The shock, which I felt for a few moments, knocked me out cold.

When I awoke, I felt no different, but relieved to be alive after the 'electrocution'. There were two more 'shocked' ones on each side of me. One was eating porridge dreamily. The other was sitting up, with a dazed and bewildered expression on her face. Her porridge was there also. There was a plate of porridge before each of us on bed-tables. It reminded me of the three bears.

A nurse came in with three mugs of tea, and bread and butter, on a tray. 'Awake, Honor? It wasn't so bad now, after all, was it? Now eat your porridge.' She took the spoon from the dazed one, who was trying to eat from the handle. She wiped it, and reversed it. 'Wrong way round, dear, that's it. Now, here's your tea.'

I had not eaten anything since six o'clock the previous evening, so I was hungry. I ate my breakfast and exchanged banalities with my fellow 'bears'.

'How do you feel?'

'Oh, not so bad, got a headache. How do you feel?'

'Can't complain. I have a slight headache, too,' I replied.

'I wish this damn treatment was over, I want to go home,' said 'Dada Bear'.

We all exchanged sympathetic glances, then we finished our breakfasts in silence.

As I dressed, I asked one of the 'regulars' had they seen Lena or

Tibby recently. I was told Lena had gone home again, three months ago, and that Tibby had left also, unexpectedly, two years ago. A widowed aunt had claimed her out, to stay with her for companionship. I exchanged greetings with the other regulars I remembered. They worked now in the kitchen – semi-paroles.

I was surprised, when I returned to Long Trench, by Nurse Best's lively attitude to my wild escape attempt. She smiled with obvious amusement.

'You really are audacious, Honor.'

'I am sorry, Nurse Best. I suddenly became terrified of the ECT.'

She patted my shoulder benevolently.

'Human weakness, Honor, that's all. However, it had to be reported, so for the rest of your treatment, two nurses will escort you over.'

Rosie came up to me. She had a mug of warm milk in one hand, and a mug of tea in the other.

'Ah! there you are, Honor. You are on "extras" from today. Sit down here with me and drink this milk, it will do you good. Nurse Best thinks you are too thin, and she put you on "extras". You will get milk now, regular, and a fried egg for your supper. Did you suffer much, darlin', from the electrocution?'

'Knocked out cold, Rosie. It's not the actual shock, but the preliminaries, the anticipation.'

'Did you have to be tied down?'

'Oh, no, Rosie, they just held me down.'

'No good can come of that sort of thing. Are you any the better for it?'

'To be truthful, Rosie, I prefer it to the insulin shock. That made me very sick.'

'Poor child, you will surely have your purgatory done here.'

'If that is right, Rosie,' I laughed, 'then you will be canonised! What age are you now?'

'Seventy-four next June.'

She was pleased at the idea of being canonised.

The next morning I went over again to the admission for ECT treatment, and for three weeks altogether, having treatment six days per week, Sundays excepted. When I had my last dose of ECT, I returned from admission for the last time to Long Trench. I met Nurse Best.

'Well, Honor, did it do you any good?'

'I can't really say, Nurse, I know absolutely nothing about electricity.'

Chapter 23

The following Monday morning I began my first day in the laundry. Nurse Goodson, the charge nurse, was a very fair, efficient person, and had taken a liking to me in advance, which I attributed to Rosie's propaganda. She showed me around the laundry and precincts herself, personally, although she was very busy. I was amazed at all the machinery and industry. Six or seven washing machines gulped down gigantic mounds of linen, cotton, etc. Some were powered by electricity, others were driven by motor, belt and wheels. Large numbers of patients were working at the beginning and the end of huge steaming sheet rollers powered by electricity. The patients at the starting point of the gigantic iron rollers put the clean damp sheets through and the patients at the receiving end folded them when dry. Other patients put them into the 'hot house', where they were thoroughly aired, and others folded them according to their marks and put them on shelves for collecting. Bath towels, chemises and nightdresses were all drying in the drying house, blowing grotesquely in the hot rushing air. A whole galaxy of men's unpressed suits frolicked and danced in the 'hot house' sometimes.

The ironing room was a big place with rows of shelves along the wall for the finished product. Two huge steam pressers were worked by patients. They were pressing uniforms and white starched coats. There were six irons, but only four patients were ironing.

'What would you like to work at, Honor?'

'What do you suggest, Nurse?'

'I think you can iron the church linen and the doctors' shirts. Of course you may do your own things here, if you wish, any time.'

It was not long until I became the top 'professional' at ironing, having to my credit tens of thousands of ironed shirts, in about ten years' work. When there was a 'special' job to be done, it was I who did it. I made pocket money from ironing ballet dresses for shows and opera shirts for 'mystery men'. The staff engaged in theatricals, and for a particular 'emergency' in raiment, I was granted a moderate fee. I had my regular work to do, continuously, but I made this pocket money with the approval of Nurse Goodson, who warned me to give no credit.

I worked in the laundry for the remainder of my time in the Big House, except for one three months when I was incapacitated. After seven years there, the continuous ironing and pressing on the revealed tendon in the palm of my hand aggravated it so much that I was forced to complain to Nurse Goodson. I told her I feared I might have to give up ironing as the pressure on the tendon was becoming unbearable. She advised me to show it to the visiting psychiatrist, who passed through the laundry twice daily. The doctor examined it, and was surprised at the complicated structure.

An appointment was made for me with the visiting surgeon, a consultant who was not on the psychiatric staff, but who called once a month to diagnose non-psychiatric phenomena.

'Ah, yes,' he said. 'Sup-tans-contraction. Yes, I think we can do something there. Can't fit her in for a month, though.' He gave me back my hand. 'All right, Honor. I will see to it.'

I told Nurse Best the surgeon would operate on my hand in a month.

'Would you like a change, Honor?' she said. 'I will suggest it to the doctor if you like – to Prospect House. You would like it there, it's a big, modern building. More leave for home from Prospect House than any other division. You never know, Honor, your friends might claim you out then.'

'I'm tired of asking them. They just ignore my appeals. Anyway, I'm all right here, I would not like to leave you. You help me a lot.'

'I have a surprise for you, Honor, I have been transferred

myself to Prospect House. I take over my new duties there in a month's time. Would that help you decide, do you think?'

'I would miss Rosie, and other friends I have made here,' I said.

'Not at all, Honor. You will see Rosie just as much. Now that you are working in the laundry, you will see Rosie and make lots of other friends too. Rosie sees you for eight hours a day now in the laundry.'

She was right, I thought. Any little step, or move at all, in the right direction, was to be grasped. And I still wanted freedom passionately and vehemently.

'What do I have to do, Nurse Best?'

'Just say to the doctor you would like a transfer. I will speak to her as well, and say you need a change. You have been long years over here, Honor.'

The psychiatrist listened attentively to my request for a transfer.

'Yes, certainly, Honor. It will be a very nice change for you. If you are sick, there is a sick dormitory there, also. You will probably have penicillin injections after the operation on your hand. Yes, it is a good idea. We do try to send surgical cases there who require convalescence.'

'Must I stay in bed?'

'No, of course not. Your hand will be dressed, and of course the injections, but you can go about for walks and messages. No work of course, but light tasks to help you.'

So it was settled, I was to go over there, beyond the little wood, to Prospect House.

Poor Rosie was downcast at first at the news. I explained that after a few weeks I would be back working in the laundry again, and see her every day. I said now that Nurse Best was going to Prospect House there was no reason why Rosie should not come over on visits. Nurse Best, I added, honoured her semi-parole as if it were a full parole. This pleased Rosie immensely, for she treated herself to a pinch of snuff as her horizon suddenly widened.

I wrote to Aunty and Paul. I said I was to have an operation on my hand, that I was changed to Prospect House, and that an application from any relative or friend now would receive instant consideration. I said I was certain I would be released in the event of an application. Paul and Aunty did write, but later, months after the operation, a myopic letter from each, and the blind spot was liberty. After reading the letters, I realised again that they had no intention of freeing me. I considered then, and always, that my long detention in the Big House was unjust and unnecessary, no matter who or what was responsible. I thought of people in prison, they at least knew their sentences. I had gone into hospital for a 'rest', and look at the 'rest' – fourteen years gone already, and very little rest at that.

Rosie used to talk about these matters. 'Your own are always the worst, dear.'

'Oh, surely not, Rosie.'

'I am an old woman, darlin', and I know, I have seen cases and cases of it . . .'

I thought, surely they must realise that there are certain occasions, as in my case, when outside help is vital, for I cannot leave, legally, without their help.

Chapter 24

Prospect House was a big, three-storeyed building, one of the few modern buildings in the Big House. On the ground level were the sick bay, a dining room, and the two day-rooms, a feature of each storey. There were fresh flowers in vases on the tables. The washing and toilet facilities were very modern. The windows were plentiful and large, and they were opened and shut by a window pole which was freely available.

I was given a single room on the third floor. There were iron stair fire escapes from each floor leading down from each dormitory. All the beds in the dormitories were vacated during the day, and any patient who fell ill went below to the sick bay. There was no observation on the higher floors, and nurses were seldom there, except for stores, baths, head combing and morning supervision of cleaning and polishing. Each patient made her own bed, and the majority of patients were mentally well, but unclaimed.

Caged shutters were on the windows of my room, but they were unlocked and swung open. All the rooms had similar fittings, but there was only one permanently locked – the detention room, below in the sick bay, which was always occupied, and only a very violent, destructive patient was left in there for a few hours, to cool off.

Poor Rosie insisted on coming up with me to see my new room.

'All these stairs, 'twould kill me,' she said.

She sat on a chair in the room while I made up my bed. I left my toilet bag, pyjamas and slippers on the bed, and the rest of my belongings I left in the case. I would put them later into my locker. Nurse Best had given me a key for a locker, with the number seven on it, for my personal belongings. Rosie surveyed the room.

'Honor, do you know, this is the room Miss Watley escaped from. Yes, I am sure it is the one.'

She peered out the window.

'How did she escape, Rosie?'

'She managed somehow, a spoon I think it was. She unscrewed or broke one of the side blocks on the window.' I looked interestedly at the blocks. It was necessary to remove one only, for the lower window to go fully up. The top window rested on the second block, and that would be unnecessary for escape.

'Anyway,' Rosie continued, 'she did it at dead of night, after the night nurse had gone on her other rounds. She goes through every two hours here. Miss Watley then, of course, had two hours' start. She knotted sheets and, clever enough, she knotted them in such a way that she had just to untie the bottom knot and she could pull the sheets down. She hid them in the graveyard, just over there. As you can guess, it was the gravedigger who found them, and they had to give him treatment over it. She was a deep one, and good luck to her, she is free now.'

'She was lucky,' I agreed.

I thought to myself, it might be worth a try, if the worst comes to the worst, but at the moment it was unnecessary even to consider it. In just over a fortnight, I would be operated on, and afterwards my hand would be bandaged, and probably in a sling.

Rosie left for Long Trench, convinced that I would be reasonably comfortable. Before she went, she promised to visit me often.

Life went on. There were eccentrics here also, in Prospect House. There was Freda. I noticed she slipped a plank each night under her mattress, before retiring. I asked her one morning what the plank was for. She laughed secretly, then giggled and finally replied with a sinister lisp:

'I kant tshay. It helpf my bawk.'

I looked at her in detail. She had a straight little figure and her back was very straight. She moved quickly, without any apparent difficulty. I asked her then, why she did not leave the plank in the bed, instead of placing it there each night.

She told me between giggles that the nurses had already found three, and then she rounded her eyes and reproached me. 'Honor, you tould know, wood is tarce.'

Clara was another eccentric. She was then the most flamboyant character of Prospect House. She was chief bottle washer in the kitchen, and helped the nurses to serve the meals, but she did her work negligently, casually, and with a laughing indifference to her surroundings. If somebody or something displeased her, she would adopt a wild western attitude. She would hitch up an imaginary six-gun belt, and drawlingly allude to her consultant as her moving target. She always shot him in the rear. Her remarks have to be censored.

Her jokes were shocking. She would commence to relate an incident with seriousness and extreme gravity, then she would explode into laughter, and include some shocking anecdote, causing her audience to emit gasps of consternation at her indelicacy. This was the case of the swill collector.

One day, according to Clara, he tried to surprise her, for when she opened the back door of the kitchen, he was outside, and *non compos mentis*. Clara insisted he was there, not for the purpose of collecting swill, but 'will'. She roared with laughter, fearing we had misconstrued her, so she described, picturesquely, for our enlightenment, his gambit, which, to put it in the queen's English, could only have been his 'exposure'. She was stopped, too late, by a very angry nurse who rebuked her for her coarseness. Clara just raised her eyebrows and laughed heartily.

Delia lived also in Prospect House. She had a single room on the second storey. There were six single rooms on each floor. Delia spent very little time in Prospect House, except for eating and sleeping there. She passed four hours in the laundry washing and ironing 'private' laundry for pocket money, but she did some things for Nurse Goodson, who then allowed her priority in other matters. She came and went as she pleased, but usually she preferred to visit her uncle. This was one of the privileges of parole, you just had to be in your division before a certain hour at night, and that was the principal clause. In the laundry I became very friendly with Delia. I found her a complex character. She puzzled both patients and staff alike. She was easily offended, especially when no offence was intended. She did not invite confidences, but she was always very accurate and discerning in her opinions.

My first month in Prospect House was drawing to a close. At last word arrived, via Nurse Best, that the ambulance would take me on the morrow to the hospital nearby for my hand operation.

It was my first operation. I was wheeled into the theatre at 10am and the operation must have taken a long time, for I was surprised when I came to to find it was the late afternoon.

I was conscious of pain first. I slowly opened my eyes and looked at my hand. It was outside the bed cover, huge, swathed in cotton wool and bandage. I moaned from the pain, and the nurse gave me a drink of water, and asked me to take a tablet to relieve the pain.

'I don't know why it hurts, Nurse,' I whispered. 'It was all right, the operation, a success, was it?'

'Yes, I was there. The pain is from the stitches. Your hand was opened up. Now try and rest, you might feel sick.'

By morning I felt much better. The surgeon came to my bedside at 11am and asked the nurse to remove the dressing. He seemed satisfied, and before I could see it properly, a fresh dressing was applied. He advised the sister in charge to leave me in bed for the day.

I had an unexpected visitor that afternoon. It was the superintendent of the Big House. He had to visit the hospital, and he thought he would look in and see how I was. I thanked him and asked if Aunty or Paul knew I had the operation. His reply was vague, non-committal, and I assumed they were uninterested in that aspect of my welfare also.

In due course the stitches were taken out, a plaster was put on, the plaster was removed, an elastic bandage was put on, and finally the wound healed. It took three months to heal. When it was time for me to go to work again, I decided to go to the sewing room for a month only. I thought sewing would be lighter work now in the beginning for therapy. I had worn a sling for months, and I wanted to use both hands together. I had become adept, while wearing the sling, at doing small tasks with my left hand, such as eating, washing, bed-making, etc. After my operation I was taken on walks, twice daily. I was also put on 'extras'. When I became a 'working patient' again, three months later, my ration of an egg for breakfast and supper and a pint of milk daily was reduced to one egg and one half pint daily. In the laundry, lots of extras were sent down to us from the staff kitchen, rashers, sausages, rice pudding and dishes of jelly and custard. I began to know what plenty was then.

But before long, life became dull and hopeless again. It was a deadly monotonous routine, of work, sleep, eat. I had the regular anti-typhoid injection every three years. I did not contract any serious illness while there, except colds, migraine and occasional depression every time I reviewed my hopeless chances of liberty. Though life was repetitive and uninspiring, I still longed for freedom, but there seemed no hope.

Chapter 25

I had by this time written thousands of letters to relatives near and far, with no results. They did not seem to speak my language. I had sewn thousands of garments, and ironed thousands of shirts, among other things, yet I seemed no nearer liberty than when I did my first day's work, gratis. I felt that my life was worse than slavery, for slaves are freed, and some buy their own freedom, by earnings, by work. I began to loathe every day of my internment.

One evening, I found an old spoon in the laundry yard. I cleaned it and kept it. The following morning at 6am in the privacy of my room, I tried it on the holding block of my window. Miss Watley the second, I thought. I put in the handle of the spoon behind the small block, and levered. To my horror, the rotten piece of wood came away all right, but in two parts, split lengthways. I concentrated on the screws. I stuck them back in their holes, but they almost fell out. I hammered them in firmly, with my shoe. This at least prevented the window from shooting up. The window was now safe, but if force was exerted I doubted if the screws would retain it. The little block of wood was too conspicuously absent to an observant person interested in such matters. If it was discovered by a nurse, for instance, or an informer, she would rightly assume I was attempting another escape. Then again, as long as it was not discovered, I would live in perpetual fear of discovery. I was not ready for escape. It was not the sheet or the plan that prevented it just now, it was the season. To correspond with the night nurse's routine and other probabilities, the ideal hour was after the mid-night, rounds, when the night was very dark, and there was no possibility of this favourable conjunction until winter or late autumn at least. It was now summer. If the window was discovered between now and winter, the least they could do would be to lock the cages, and I would be a caged animal again. The worst they could do, initially, would be to have me transferred back to the Hold. Whatever the consequences, I would lose the new status I had acquired now, of reliable worker.

All these thoughts raced through my mind as I gathered up the split block from the floor. I decided to try and find a similar block of wood to replace it. I took a wooden coat hanger from my case. I wanted to break off a suitable piece, to look like a block temporarily. I managed finally to replace the block of wood by a wooden, banana-shaped imitation. I looked up at it critically, and I actually walked up three or four times to the window, to get an unbiased impression. I thought, at least it is wood, whole, and the window cannot shoot up suddenly.

One false move though! All was ready now, the difficult part anyhow, for the escape. A very dark night, tie the double sheets from the iron bedstead, climb down, untie the knot, pull down the sheets, and *fait accompli*!

Prospect House was full of informers, so I resolved to allow nobody into my room, even to chat, if I could help it. I could make my bed, dust and polish the room myself and lock it before going to the laundry. Aware that the banana-shaped piece of wood would not bear close scrutiny, I kept a lookout for a more suitable block of wood all summer. Freda's plank of wood was a board of irony to me now, and her secret giggles exasperating.

I asked frequently to accompany the nurse on the messages, hoping for a find. One day I was lucky. She had to call at the carpentry shop, about the return of repaired chairs, and she also had to collect paint and floor polish. The nurse and the attendant went out to the yard behind the shop, and I was left alone inside, with Ice-Blue. I determined to waste no time.

'Hello, could I have a small piece of wood?'

He seemed to come out of a trance. 'Certainly. What sort of wood do you want?'

I walked past him, my eyes roving the floor and the bare

benches, seeking a suitable similar piece to the original. He followed me slowly, pondering.

'Do you want it for something in particular?' he enquired.

'Yes . . . I was thinking of, whittling, you know . . . it helps, if you want to learn wood-carving,' I compromised desperately.

'I see,' he said.

I knew he did not.

'Well, look around, take what you want,' he said. I was doing that, but curly shavings and boards were all I could see. Then the nurse and the attendant came in and I sighed and resigned myself to the coathanger.

As we left I said loudly to Ice-Blue, for the staff's benefit, 'See you at the dance, then. Cheerio.'

I was in it now, up to my two ears. Each evening when I returned tired and weary from the laundry, I would suddenly rush up the three flights of stairs and look through the glass panel of my door, to see if the shutters were locked. Then, satisfied that all was as it should be, I would go to the dining hall for my supper. Terra firma, but still anxious and half expecting a dreaded summons to the office and orders to go to the Hold.

My suspense was brought to an end six weeks later, towards the end of autumn.

I was in bed. It was about one hour to 'lights out'. I was reading a cowboy western novel. In the bookcase of Prospect House there were two kinds of books – mystery stories and western stories. Of the two, I preferred the former, but I had read them all, except the western story I was now reading. Clara had read it and said, hedonistically, that it was 'the goods'. I was just in the middle of a feudal range war when there was a knock at the door. A nurse came in, in 'civvies'. I knew her from the admission days.

'Hello, Honor, I thought I would pay you a visit.'

She sat on the chair beside my bed, directly beneath the 'botched' block. I silently prayed she would not look up at it. My heart was thumping, for she was one of the suspicious, observant ones.

'This is a surprise,' I managed to reply casually. 'What brings you out so late at night?'

I left down the open book on the bed.

'I thought I'd look in to see how you're getting along. Working in the laundry?'

'Yes, I am quite a professional ironer now.'

She looked up at the window, and jumped to her feet.

'Honor, your window, the block, it seems to be . . .'

'Broken?' I replied casually. 'Yes, I noticed that, but then it doesn't open.'

'It's against all the rules. I shall have to report it.'

'If you like, I will report it in the morning,' I forced a laugh, 'it will last another day.'

She considered and made a decision.

'I will see Nurse Best tonight. I'm surprised it went unnoticed.'

I heard Matron coming, by auditory indications outside, and told her. She left hurriedly, as I guessed she would, for she was not on duty, and nurses off duty always avoid the matron.

After breakfast the next morning I was summoned to Nurse Best's office. She was smiling, pleasant and amiable as usual.

'Honor, Nurse Daniel told me your window block is broken. I will have the carpenter repair it today. Make sure your room is tidy, Honor.'

And that was all. No suspicions, no accusations. I decided not to go to the laundry, and when the laundry nurse called for the workers I pleaded a headache. I wanted to remove the coat hanger before he found it, for he would know. I threw it in the dustbin.

Ice-Blue was sent to repair the damage. He had in his hand a hammer, screws, and an identical window block. I met him near the room. A nurse was with him. He was smiling to himself and although he said nothing, I think he knew what had happened.

'I'll show you the window,' I said.

He repaired the damage in about three minutes, and left, smiling, hurried away by the nurse, to repair another installation.

It was over. My winter plans for escape were blocked, literally, and I might even be suspect. I had got off scot-free apparently. If I had been sent back to the Hold again, I felt I might really have gone mad.

Chapter 26

That was my last attempt to escape. Two years later the superintendent retired and a new superintendent took over, and with his coming things changed for the better. Rumours were floating about, weeks before the final break – wild revellings in the sacrosanct demesne of the superintendent, multiple farewell parties, secret orgies, fabulous presentations, were some of them – before it was finally ascertained that he was leaving. A final farewell board meeting was held to celebrate the auspicious occasion. For two days he said goodbye to us all, individually and collectively, until 'the last dry and twisted tube' was forsaken. The pasha had finally retired and had left us to his unknown successor.

There now beat in the muffled drums of all hearts the curious and exciting questions – 'Who? When? What?'

New dresses and suits were hastily doled out, by the hundreds, and exclamations were fast and furious.

'For goodness' sake, Matilda, will you stand still and let me put this lovely dress on you. There is a new superintendent coming to see you.'

Tilly refused.

'The last time the inspector came, you gave me a new dress, and when he was gone you took it off again.'

'Yes, it is for special occasions. If you didn't slop your food, you could keep it!' The question of what 'his form' was was finally answered by the announcement that he had arrived, and was even now on his way through the various departments to see his patients. On his first day of sight-seeing Matron accompanied him on the female rounds. Similar precautions were adopted on the male rounds. Matron introduced him to one or two patients, here and there, praising them for good behaviour, excellent work, etc, and many patients attempted to introduce themselves. He was clever, for he avoided handshaking by keeping his hands in his pockets.

I noticed how different he was, even in appearance, to the previous superintendent. He was chubby, and his face and hair shone. Unlike the other super, he used hair-oil, which suited his glowing, beaming, soap-washed face. The old super must have used talcum after shaving, for his face was always dry and cynical. This man's eyes were a soft brown, and they were beaming, smiling. He could be called jovial, but never jocular. He never wore a waistcoat, but his open jacket and trousers were superbly tailored. He wore them, though, as if he were looking for a salami, whereas the other superintendent wore his as if he expected a salaam. He was fatherly, which might satisfy certain complexes. It was impossible for me to realise then that this affable man, who never insisted on psychiatric obscurity, was to be my liberator.

Meanwhile I thought glum thoughts. Wait until he reads my records, the disproportionate, fantastic, exaggerated headlines of my misdeeds. Rosie said she had seen four supers there in her day, and that the first thing they do is to give paroles, to express their goodwill. About a dozen, Rosie considered.

'A dozen, out of three thousand patients?'

'Now, darlin', don't be discouraged, ask him for a parole. He will or he will not.'

'When he reads my case-history, from what I know of certain nurses, and staff imagination and expression . . . what do you think of him, Rosie?'

'Time will tell. I heard from one of the maids that he is very easy-going. Wait and see. I heard just recently that "conditions" will improve in places like this soon. Why, even now, Honor, over in the admission, I believe patients there are coming and going as they please. "Voluntary" they call it.'

'It is too late for me, Rosie. I would have been voluntary, as I just needed a rest, but that time, Rosie, there was no such thing as the Voluntary Patients Act or whatever they call it.'

Rosie speculated on its advantages.

'Ah! Once a woman knows she can come in voluntary like that, Honor, husbands, relations, are powerless to . . . to . . .'

'Stop her jumping her fences before she comes to them. Rosie, the great majority of patients here were victimised, calumniated, and some were put in for spite. Anyhow the Voluntary Patients Act does not solve my problems. Both my parents are dead, my home is sold, and my only brother refuses to claim me out, and he is not legally compelled to do so.'

'Look on the bright side, darlin', good days are coming, mark my words.'

Good days did come. It was almost impossible to have an interview with the superintendent, so in a manner of speaking, 'I let my bed down through the roof'. I wrote to him. It was more or less private, too, because a letter to the superintendent goes uncensored from the office. I decided to plead my sanity first with him, and then to ask him what solution there was, if any, to my particular problem. I explained everything to him in letters, and one day in the laundry he told me he was considering what could be done. I gave him my brother's address, on his request. Two months later he said he had written to my brother twice, requesting an application, but had had no reply. I confessed then that the other superintendent had also written him without result.

He thought, and he seemed angry.

'I may have another solution to your problem, Honor.'

I thought how different the psychology of the two superintendents! The first, when snubbed by my brother's non-replying, accepted with a fatalistic shrug the inevitable, but not the new super – it was a challenge.

I had to wait three more years before I heard something to my advantage. In those last three years, I felt more hopeful, for the superintendent had taken part of the burden from me by his attitude, by his talks, brief though they were, and usually in the laundry where I worked. He had admitted, also, that I should not have stayed more than a year in the Big House.

Gradually, imperceptibly, improvements and changes were

introduced, weekly, monthly, until one day I realised that the man-
acles were being shattered one by one. It was far from perfect, but
people in high places were intent on good works.

We now had a mixed patients' social club. We met thrice
weekly. The monthly dance now became a weekly affair. There was
dancing every Sunday afternoon, and a relaxing concert in the
evening. A very small percentage of the patients joined the social
club in the beginning, but as time went on the number increased.
Dancing became the popular recreation, with almost half of the
patients attending regularly. The social club organised croquet,
clock-golf, tournaments in the summer. In the winter there were
walks, whist drives, sing-songs, and Christmas carol practice.
Allowances for pensioners were increased, and Rosie now had
extra snuff, and even the odd cigarette she occasionally indulged
in multiplied. Any money I had I earned in the laundry, five
shillings for a bad week and ten shillings for the average. The
nurses paid me a small fee to iron and press their dance frocks. I
often did the odd opera shirt for the old eccentrics, too, for the
odd remuneration. I was not paid for my daily work in the
laundry, nobody was.

One day in the laundry, the superintendent called me. 'Your
chance, Honor, it's come,' he said.

My heart jumped. What could he mean?

He explained in detail. A new rehabilitation centre had been
opened, and he had been requested to send two or three of his
patients there. He said he had selected me, and another patient
from the admission and another from No. 4 division.

I was overjoyed. In fact I could not believe it. Liberty in view at
last, authorised freedom! I said, with random exhilaration: 'At last!
May I really leave here? My relations cannot stop me? They don't
count?'

'Not as far as I am concerned,' he said.

Sincerely I thanked him. I was almost incoherent with joy and
excitement.

'Shall I write and tell them, must they sign a form or something . . .'

'No! I am taking full responsibility for you. You will be trained there, in some occupation, then after a year, you will be offered employment through the rehabilitation agency. Then you are free, Honor.'

'Free? Really? Thank you, thank you . . .'

'You will very soon be interviewed by a committee of social workers, psychiatrists and doctors. It is only a preliminary essential. I am certain you will qualify.'

'Oh yes, Doctor, I don't mind interviews at all. I have just got to, or else, no freedom.'

He smiled confidently.

'You will be free, Honor, I will give you more details later.'

I almost believed in fairy tales again. I was bursting to tell the good news to Rosie, Delia, Oonagh, Nurses Best, Goodson, everyone I knew. Soon, it was an accepted fact that I and two others had been chosen to go for rehabilitation. We were the pioneers of a new movement that would surely gather momentum and free hundreds inside in the future years.

I thought Rosie would be sad and lonely when I told her where I was going.

'Thank God, child. I knew He would help. Slow but sure, He is.' She gave me lots of advice. 'Don't ever come back, or think about it. It is very hard, almost impossible to get out again – you understand?'

'Don't worry about that, Rosie, I never want to see a hospital again.'

'And keep away from your relations, child. They would not raise a hand to save you. Remember they left you here to die. "Your own are always the worst",' she said sadly.

'Yes, Rosie, I will. I will get a job and be independent. Do you remember that saying, Rosie?'

'What was that, darlin'?'

'You said – love many, trust few, always paddle your own canoe.

'Aye, that's a true saying.'

Afterword
to 1987 edition

Many people will remember Hanna Greally's appearance on the *Late Late Show* shortly after *Bird's Nest Soup* was first published in 1971. Specialists who met Hanna at the time thought that she would have problems 'staying out' of the Big House for the rest of her life because of the effects of institutionalisation, grief and loneliness.

Not only did Hanna 'make it', but, until overtaken by physical ill health a few years ago, she managed to paddle her own canoe rather well. She gained her independence a year after leaving Mullingar Mental Hospital and went from strength to strength, give or take a few of life's little slings and arrows. Highly employable, she worked in Ireland before going to England, and wrote three full-length manuscripts, many short stories, and poetry. And she learned how to love and grieve and start all over again, abilities which surely must be included in any definition of mental health. Hanna worked as a cook house-keeper, a job description which, in her case, is not a euphemism for the untrained work that is supposed to come 'naturally' to a woman when she is not trained for anything else. She was highly qualified. She had trained hard and graduated with honours as a person capable of running the grandest house. It was nothing to Hanna to whip up a French menu or prepare a banquet.

Hanna Greally is respected in Roscommon by friends and neighbours. She has good women friends who readily admit to being exasperated by some of her ways, but they are loyal and fond of her. She has never paid men much heed, and it seems to be a fairly common male opinion that Hanna is 'too intelligent', 'has too many brains for her own good'. Hanna is different, everyone agrees, but by no means 'daft' and, indeed, if she were unbalanced after all she has been through nobody would blame her. After getting out of the Big House, life was never easy; memories, insecurity and loneliness stalked her days.

Years ago, long before she had had her nervous breakdown, Hanna was seen as different in Athlone, where she grew up. She walked beside the Shannon at 6am, and wrote beautiful poetry which was published in the *Westmeath Independent*. And she was beautiful: 'She was tall and willowy, walked like a spring-heeled Johnny,' says her childhood next-door neighbour, Eithne Fallon, now Eithne Quinn and a Roscommon councillor. 'She had lovely auburn hair down her back, you'd love to look at her, and she still has those big blue eyes. In Athlone all eyes were on Hanna, she went to the Bowers Convent, and played hockey for the town as well as the school team.'

Hanna's mother was one of the wealthy Murrays of Athlone. Her grandmother had been a great businesswoman, but Baby Murray, Hanna's mother, was not. The Murrays had lots of property and a fine grocery business with a bar. It was on a corner with two corner doors and a fine terrazzo floor; Councillor Quinn described it in detail in an effort to impress its substantiality upon me. Hanna's mother was an heiress.

Baby Murray, who in the tradition of the West of Ireland was never called anything but Baby, being the youngest of the family, married James Greally, a travelling tea-salesman. They had a prominent social profile in Athlone. Eithne Quinn's mother and father used to be invited to dinner parties at Greallys' along with writer John Broderick's parents, and Baby dazzled her guests with her high fashion gowns. They would sit down to a perfect meal served by 'Carrie', who was dressed in black sateen with a little lace collar.

The marriage was only about six years old when James Greally died suddenly, leaving two children, Hanna and her brother. From then on, Baby Greally appears to have been robbed blind by people with better business heads than her own. Friends and neighbours watched, horrified, as the Murrays' wealth slipped through Baby's fingers, and kept running until there was nothing left.

As a teenager, the brilliant Hanna got her entrance exam to Trinity College, Dublin, although she did not take it up, probably because there was not enough money for her to do so. She went to Guy's Hospital in London, to train as a nurse. She did well, and in due course moved to another London hospital, which was bombed. Hanna came back to Ireland. At home, unnerved by that experience, Hanna faced the reality that her once rich mother was now incredibly poor. Hanna idolised her mother, but may have resented the fact that Baby Murray had lost the family fortune, and mother and daughter seem to have run into the teenage rebellion stage of Hanna's development. The girl's being 'difficult' was aggravated by her having been bombed out in London, and by the impoverishment, which, bright as Hanna was, must have struck her as something that need never have happened; from what I have learned about Hanna, it seems obvious that had *she* been the heiress, the family fortune would have been well managed. The nervous breakdown became too much for the mother and daughter to handle, and it was agreed that Hanna needed a rest and nursing care. There was no money, and Hanna's mother committed her only daughter to Mullingar Mental Hospital. When, eventually, Hanna improved and was ready to go home, her mother was ill, then suddenly dead.

There is nothing about those terrible years in the Big House that I could paint more vividly than Hanna has done in *Bird's Nest Soup*. For me, the most startling lines of her story are when Hanna writes: 'A few more years passed.' And she does it more than once. A few more years . . . written of someone enduring minute after minute in such a place, someone who was not too ill to know or care where she was, not too numbed to realise that she was trapped, never too passive to give up her fight for freedom. Hanna's 'difficult' ways were used against her, to warrant treating her as the 'insane' were treated then. Again and again reading her book, I was impressed by Hanna's 'normality'. As she was being punished, despised or drugged for her behaviour, I was bound to ask myself, yet again: 'How did they expect her to behave in those circumstances?'

Even when her mother died, taking with her to the grave her daughter's hope of liberty, not to mention any healing resolution that might have happened between the two women, Hanna was patted down. She was not allowed to go to her mother's funeral. Medical specialists are always saying how important it is for the bereaved to confront the trauma of the funeral. We now know that for many people who do not attend the funeral of a loved one, the loss never actually happens for them, so that grieving is impaired, causing pathology later on.

Nor was Hanna encouraged to grieve, to hang in there with the pain. Nobody sat with her. It is a long time ago, and I would not emphasise it were it not for the fact that so many so-called 'experts' on human feelings would do the same today. Hand out Valium. Hush now. Go to sleep. They drugged Hanna. She was given hot milk to wash down something that kept her insensible in her bed. Eventually, the drugs gained control of Hanna's feelings, and she was able to return to her everyday hell.

In reading Hanna's other writings, I became aware of the toll which that unresolved grief took of her, and wondered how much the unfinished business of grieving over her father's death might have had a part in her later breakdown. *Bird's Nest Soup* shows up so clearly that, as long as the institution ran smoothly, the patient was of secondary consideration. To some extent, this is still true today, even though the human dynamics of an institution are better understood. In Hanna's day, the 'good' patient was the one who behaved, fitted in, did not interfere with nursing routine. This was, of course, the sort of patient who could be forgotten. A lot of the disturbance in mental hospitals then (I am told by psychiatrists) was an attempt to be noticed, to compel people to recognise that one was a *person*. Hanna Greally was not about to let people forget she was there, and she kept on kicking up about her liberty as best she could, until she got out.

The word 'asylum' is shivered over by Hanna, but it is a favourite word of mine because of its connotation of rescue. It is a kind word, in my opinion, suggesting shelter and offering some kind of refuge to those who are homeless, helpless. The mental hospital evolved from the asylum, which, in turn, evolved out of

Ireland's post-famine needs when so many impoverished, home-less people, unable to emigrate, crowded outside soup kitchens, into workhouses, or slept rough. The so-called 'Big House' often offered asylum for those who slept rough or were starving. Until recently, there was always a proportion of mental hospital beds kept for people who starkly needed asylum.

This function of giving asylum has gradually eroded over the years, and may soon be lost for ever. The question of whether the homeless belong in the 'Big House' seems to be beside the point when one realises how glad of a warm bed in a mental hospital many of Ireland's homeless can be, when they succeed in gaining admission. For years, the mental hospitals had partly succeeded in shaking off the Poor Law atmosphere to which Hanna was sub-jected, but now, with radical cuts in expenditure on health services in the 1980s, it would seem as if it must come full circle, with serv-ices provided for the poor at the lowest possible public expenditure.

The lengths to which Poor Law treatment of the needy went to save money were illustrated to me recently when Dr Joseph Fernandez, a Dublin psychiatrist deeply concerned with the homeless, recalled that it was not long ago since patients were not permitted to shave themselves. Nurses shaved the men, but they were bound to do so economically and to account for a certain number of shaves per blade. 'Good' patients or favourites got shaved first, and the others had to suffer a blunt blade. There was no furniture for patients, and they had to roll their few clothes for use as a pillow. They placed the legs of the bed in their shoes so that the latter would not be swiped as they slept.

Women were not allowed mirrors then, although, in private psychiatric clinics of the time, women were exhorted by nurses to 'tart themselves up' as a signal of improving health looked for by the doctors. I recently met a woman who had a friend bring her make-up in hospital, because she was afraid that her doctor would not believe she was 'trying' unless she 'did herself up for him'. She did not use make-up before she went to hospital, and has not used it since her discharge.

And while some things have changed in relation to mental illness, a lot remains the same. In spite of the new forms of treatment, when it comes to attitudes we have a long way to go. After all, if the public attitude to mental illness was one of accept- ance, psychiatric care would not still be the Cinderella of the public health service; people would not tolerate this state of affairs. However, the public is still only too ready to banish the mentally ill out of sight, into anyone else's care. It is as if the community externalises its own pathology by disconnecting itself from those members who *express* its insanity.

But could it happen now? Could a modern Hanna find herself held in hospital indefinitely? No. For the simple reason that the emphasis is now on a form of community care which counts success in terms of empty hospital beds. The thrust now is to avoid providing asylum at all costs to those who need it. However, it seems relatively easy to convince a psychiatrist that one is 'sick' if one has a mind to. In the famous Rosenhand experiment in the U.S. some years ago, *On Being Sane in Insane Places*, a team of people gained admission to hospitals in one area, and were labelled 'query schizophrenic'. The symptom presented by each 'patient' was what she or he described as a 'lub dub' noise in the head, which refused to go away. The impersonators were treated as 'sick', and when they owned up to their 'normality', the result was a drop in hospital admissions for some time afterward; patients were now suspect, and were sent away for fear that they were not really ill.

After the Second World War, the care of the mentally ill in Europe and America started moving rapidly away from the methods of treatment and attitudes of the past. New drugs seemed miraculous, lifting depression and soothing anxiety, and psy- chotherapy introduced a new atmosphere of closeness between doctor and patient. There were also changes in the law which pro- tected patients' rights. There were doctors now who only wanted to be proven right in their belief that, given half a chance, many patients could be restored to a full life in the community. Such doctors did a lot to change attitudes to mental illness, and the walls of overt oppression which surrounded so many mentally ill people began to crumble. Doors were unlocked, patients allowed out, social life allowed in, and people in mental hospitals were encouraged to hope.

The new Registered Medical Superintendent of Mullingar Mental Hospital, to whom Hanna wrote a letter pleading her sanity, was Dr Finn O'Brien. In Castlerea, before arriving in Mullingar, he had been the first to create an open hospital. He was a founder member of the Mental Health Association of Ireland. Dr O'Brien chose Hanna to be among the pioneers of female rehabilitation in Ireland, and sent her to the newly opened Coolamber House in Co. Longford.

Hanna's time in Coolamber was sheltered, a kindly, encouraging environment in which she learned skills to help her face the world again. In the sixties, she published an eight-part series in the *Roscommon Champion* describing her rehabilitation in the new place. Her arrival at Coolamber from the Big House must have seemed too good to be true, and she described the lovely house, the friendly welcome, the beautiful grounds, in an atmosphere golden with hope: 'I was introduced to my room-mates and I like them. After tea, we were shown the college and grounds. Pain and suffering had brought us together.' Students at Coolamber had disabilities of all kinds, and Hanna's series showed the development of many people who might have been thrown on the scrap-heap, or allowed to rot in well-meaning care, growing ever more dependent as time passed. She told of a one-handed youth who ploughed and sowed and planted Coolamber until a farmer's paradise emerged. She wrote of the privilege (and elitism) of being in that first Group A, and the intensity of the training. Her independent spirit seems to have flourished there from day one.

She wrote a most detailed account of life at Coolamber in its first year. There was the new bus that drove the fourteen women everywhere, and their flighty young bachelor-driver who fell in love with one after the other of them. Hanna cycled everywhere and only resorted to the bus when the weather was dubious and she was going over five miles. She described the courage of the other students, the slimming craze at Coolamber; one can see how her team spirit increased as the weeks and seasons passed, as did her desire for liberty.

And then before Christmas, everyone except Hanna was getting ready to go somewhere for the holiday. An officer at Coolamber asked her what she would like to do. 'I would like to stay a week in Dublin at a hotel,' replied Hanna, 'go to pantomimes, rest, go to museums, art galleries and the zoo.' He said he would see what he could do. A few days later, he told Hanna that 'rehabilitation' would book her for a week at a good hotel. She describes the perfection of the first Christmas dinner held at Coolamber a week before they broke up for the holidays. I've cooked many a turkey in my life, but never knew you could remove the leg sinews the way Hanna learned to do at Coolamber.

Alone in Dublin, and armed with a box of chocolates, Hanna went to the pantomime *Goody Two Shoes*, visited St. Martin's Moving Crib on Christmas Eve, and lit her own Christmas candle in her room. She attended three masses on Christmas Day. Lonely Hanna? Perhaps, but it was her first bit of real freedom after all those years, and on Christmas Day she was invited to two parties. After the Easter holidays, spent with a cousin, there was the summer exam term. Coolamber was mainly a domestic training college, and the students had to choose whether they wanted to cook, housekeep, be waitresses or confectioners or poultry girls. She fancied the confectionery, but it would take another year and Hanna was impatient for freedom: 'Again and again I thought of liberty. I would soon be a citizen, I would vote, earn money, even do crosswords and perhaps, become well off,' she wrote. She graduated with honours, her skills including the milking and maintenance of ten cows and ten calves, and in the month of August she left Coolamber for her first job. She was to remember Coolamber as 'never without flowers. Prize roses preened against grey walls, exuding perfume and luxury.'

It certainly wasn't all roses for Hanna after she left Coolamber. Still, her first job was in a suburb near the sea, and her dream of liberty had always featured walks amidst sea breezes. Her first boss seems to have been odder than Hanna was permitted to be in the Big House, and very unreasonable to say the least, and the next employer kept a lock on the freezer, doling out the food.

It was a changed world for Hanna. She had no relatives near, friends had married and lost touch with her. 'Commerce was now the key-note to success,' she wrote of Sean Lemass's mohair-suited sixties. However, in common with all other women, Hanna did not have a mohair suit. They were for 'the boys', and there were mini-skirts everywhere. 'Television was new in Ireland and one half knew what the other half was thinking.' She recalls that 'the public was insatiable for change, for revolution, for speed. Natural disasters seemed more terrible now when reporting was coupled with viewing, as on television, and called "live".' News had been 'canned' when she was young and now on television she saw the assassination of John F. Kennedy. She was alone and felt that she could not explain to people about where she had been and why. And so she began writing *Bird's Nest Soup*.

Hanna was looking for another job when a relative strongly advised her to go to a visiting agency who 'were in town to recruit rejected girls for the emigrant ships'. The relative spoke in 'prejudicial despair' of Hanna finding work again in Ireland. It was only in retrospect that she realised that in his view she was a despicable common domestic, while all his family were social aspirants. It was for the sake of his family honour that the man so strongly urged emigration. He reminded her that she would have anonymity and prosperity abroad. She had never sought either, merely looked for a little happiness and a stable livelihood. Again, she felt nobody cared; she was being banished.

Hanna had several good jobs in England before she went to housekeep for Dr Joseph, retired in Surrey. Her years there were the golden ones. She became friends with the postwoman, among others, and they went together to see the Russian Ballet. She toured around England when she could, developed a full life with friends and had plenty to occupy her. And then the gentle Dr Joseph had a heart attack, after which Hanna was loath to leave him alone for any reason.

Dr Joseph's was her last post in England. Hanna was with him for the six years prior to his death. As well as her employer, he was her dearest friend. 'But when Joseph died, I died too,' wrote Hanna in a manuscript. 'Part of me survives, the part of the wounded, scarred lover, who disguised her love with loyal care, and practical service, part companion, part domestic, when all the intrusions of common chores and domestic duties were no more, on that sad "end of the world" day, while rose trees bloomed with fragrant love in his garden, at his home, outside my kitchen window.'

Hanna was inconsolable. She disconnected her radio and television and was aware that she wept old tears along with the new: 'I wept for the beauty of the world, that was not for him and not for me, and all the loss of the past and the loves that were dead, all, all died again without me.'

Hanna took care of Dr Joseph's home for a few months until the family sold it, and then she came back to Ireland, homeless and loath to face another employer. She had a rest and took a job in a crumbling Irish castle. Some time later, *Bird's Nest Soup* was published and Hanna appeared on the *Late Late Show*. Excellent though it is, the book did not make Hanna much money then, and she was conscious of people knowing that she had been 'you know where' after she appeared on T.V. However, a British magazine had serialised *Bird's Nest Soup*, and Dr Joseph's family had given her £100 as a parting gift. Scraping all she had together, Hanna bought an old vested cottage in Roscommon.

She called it 'Sunny Acre'. The floorboards were rotten and she took them up and made gates of them, laying cement floors. Set in a meadow, the cottage overlooks the Lake of the Birds, but, says a friend: 'Didn't Hanna put up venetian blinds and keep them closed. I don't know what she could have been thinking of to do that.' As someone else remarked, wasn't it her window and her view and her venetian blinds, and Hanna must be well used to her friends forever trying to find a key to her thinking.

She had a good life in her little cottage, with plenty of visitors, but in recent years Hanna has been plagued by ill health. She has lost most of her fingers because of gangrene, caused by a circulatory disease which landed her in hospital again in 1987, and she was forced to leave 'Sunny Acre' because she was unable to manage there after she burned her foot. It was extremely difficult to prise Hanna from her cottage.

Reading the manuscripts of her life, talking to people who knew her, it is clear that if women got awards for survival, Hanna Greally is overdue hers. Now, she has friends who care about her, even though they might despair of understanding her. She was always different, that's the marvellous thing about Hanna. And she has done the soldier saint, after whom she was named, proud, triumphing equally as well as Joan in the battle for her identity. And was not Joan of Arc also described as a 'very difficult' maiden? Or, to put it like Hanna's West of Ireland neighbours, 'bould as brass, but not daft by any means'.

June Levine, August 1987

Postscript

This piece was on its way to the printers when Hanna Greally, christened Joanna, died in Roscommon County Hospital on Saturday, 15 August 1987, at 1pm. She had plenty of visitors during her last, brief, illness, some friends having come far and stayed long with her. Had Hanna lived, there is no doubt that she would have been cruelly physically disabled.

Hanna left her mark on the world by the example of her living. Having lost her liberty at the age of nineteen, she valued it above all else, knowing that freedom was easily lost, but not so easily held. When her childhood friend rang to tell me that 'Joan' was gone, I thought again of that other Joan who fought so hard for her identity, her integrity. She could have given in, given up, pretended she was what they wanted her to be, but how could she, loving truth and liberty? We can say the same of Hanna Greally, who was always true to herself, and expressed her sense of self and wholeness in everything she did. Hanna is a hero of our times, and her story will, I know, inspire younger women to put as high a value on their own lives as she did on hers.

Nor did Hanna intend to surrender her identity in death. When she worked in England during the sixties, she bought herself a plot in Dublin's Dean's Grange Cemetery. She did not want to be buried in exile. A couple of years ago, when money was short, friends suggested to Hanna that she sell the plot. In any case, they said, Dublin was a long distance to go for a funeral. 'Sure, I have free travel,' said Hanna Greally. The toast, sisters, is 'Difficult Women'.

Afterword
to 1971 edition

The Big House was not a criminal asylum, where detention is compulsory, but an ordinary provincial mental hospital. Some long-term patients there still call it, bitterly, the asylum. The old, fresh, moist, institutional web still envelops their dreams and memories. There, cheats are cheated, frauds are defrauded, and life, for some, is suspended in horror, sorrow, blissful rapport, or sublimation. I see myself now, free, yet I often think, sometimes sadly, of the friends I made there – the outcasts, the unloved, the incurably embittered, and the spirited, still fighting for their liberty. Some may be insane, in the psychiatric sense of that word, but I feel certain that many hundreds would be more normal if they were rehabilitated, by charitable people, or organisations. It would take understanding, patience, but more often a sense of humour, to assist and re-educate them to make the best of themselves. Some patients lived twenty, thirty, forty years in the Big House. In their day work was not plentiful, and families were only too glad to shift their responsibilities on to the state, in some cases permanently. After long years there without love or hope, many patients deteriorated from their original personalities, and became introverted so completely that they shunned all reality. Others turned completely to God, and fortunately there was a chapel there, and a chaplain and minister, to assist and console the lonely. Some patients died, with nobody to care. Sometimes they were visited on their death beds, which might be the only occasion that they had visitors. Some even in death were alone, unclaimed perhaps, or without living relatives, and these were buried in the hospital graveyard, with only little numbered wooden crosses above the anonymous graves.

Some tried to escape at dead of night, on sheets from windows, but they were usually recaptured at their homes, or en route. Although the Big House was not hell for everybody, it was definitely limbo for most poor souls.

While many were dying of broken hearts, others, more despairing, were attempting suicide, slashing their wrists with a jealously guarded piece of delph or broken glass they had stumbled upon on the exercise walks. Slashing was unusual, but when it happened, it was nearly always a bungled affair, an act of open defiance or a last desperate bid for freedom. These, and all such despairing acts, only further alienated them from official sympathy, who reported and recorded such lapses as 'serious'. Precautions were taken then, to preserve the threatened security inside. Security became the chief aim after an escape, and any indication of rebellion on a patient's part was punished by injections, bed and lack of privileges. Many were immune to punishment, were not easily provoked, and went on their harmless way, intent on their secret plans. Everybody had plans of some sort, but nobody could discuss them for there were always two or three informers in their own midst, who sought favours and, to ingratiate themselves with the staff, they appointed themselves as censors of their other unfortunate comrades, who asked no favours, only truth.

Twenty years is a long time. When I came back to work in the world, I found that all my old friends had gone, married, emigrated. My relatives discuss me, I know, as an embarrassing resurrection.

Hanna Greally, 1971